"We're all stewards of the time, abilities, and opportunities God has entrusted to us. But how do we steward these well when there are so many distractions and so many drains on our focus and energy? Ana Ávila shows us how in this simple yet profound book. Ávila applies godly wisdom to living out our ordinary days on purpose so that we can avoid not only wasting our time but wasting our lives."

Nancy Guthrie, author; Bible teacher

"Ana Ávila's enthusiasm for productivity for Jesus's sake is contagious. She takes into account both our eternally focused goals and our earthbound, creaturely limitations. This book is a refreshing and friendly coach for readers who want to make the most of the time they've been given."

Gloria Furman, author, *Labor with Hope and Missional Motherhood*

"I have never read a book on productivity until now. Learning about planning, scheduling, and goal setting was as appealing to me as it is for a young child to go to the doctor for a shot. I am a classic improviser. How helpful it would have been to read this little treasure twenty years ago! I love how Ávila weaves the gospel into every page—she makes it clear to us that productivity isn't about achieving but loving. I finished this book confident that God accepts me because of Christ's perfect performance and that as I grow in awe of this truth, I will pour out my love to him and it will be seen in how I use my time."

Aixa de López, author, *Forever: What Adoption Teaches Us about the Father's Heart*

"In *Make the Most of Your Productivity*, Ana Ávila provides us with a precise definition of productivity, the proper motivation to support productivity, and a variety of practical tools that can help us grow in our productivity not only for our own sake but also for the sake of others. She does so in a way that is profound in theology yet simple in application. Everyone should read this book in order to learn how to better manage the most valuable resource they have: time."

Cole Brown, author *The Gospel Is: Defining the Most Important Message in the World*

"A lot of writing on productivity lacks personal introspection and focuses more on tasks than motives. In this book, Ana Ávila offers us a treasure that not only helps us with productivity-related actions but also helps us reflect on the whys and therefores of our productivity. Ávila reminds us that productivity is first and foremost a matter of loving God and neighbor. If you can't focus on what you should, this book is for you. If you think productivity is simply 'getting a lot done,' this book is for you. If you think productivity isn't important to God, this book is also for you. It is for every person who wants to make good use of their life for the glory of God and the good of their neighbor."

Justin Burkholder, author, *Sobre la roca: Un modelo para iglesias que plantan iglesias*

"Wise people follow good advice, but fools say they will do things and never follow through. I thank God for the wisdom he has given Ana Ávila because she has not only been able to listen to good advice but has also put it into practice. And now, with humility and skill, she has written a book that is suggested (even required!) reading for Christians who want to do God's will in their work and daily life. However, there is something else. I sense that this book can be of vital help to churches and ministries that want to honor God in ways that have measurable results. Of course, the things we do are secondary to who we are, but as Ávila shows us in this book, if we want to glorify God with all that we are, we will seek to be wise in all that we do. May God raise up more authors to serve the church. I am already looking forward to reading the next book from Ávila's pen."

Jairo Namnún, Executive Director, Coalición por el Evangelio

Make the Most of Your Productivity

Make the Most of Your Productivity

A Guide to Honoring God with Your Time

Ana Ávila

CROSSWAY®

WHEATON, ILLINOIS

Make the Most of Your Productivity: A Guide to Honoring God with Your Time

© 2024 by Ana Ávila

Published by Crossway
           1300 Crescent Street
           Wheaton, Illinois 60187

Originally published as *Aprovecha bien el tiempo* (2020) by the Nelson Group in Nashville, Tennessee, United States of America. Used by permission. Published by arrangement with HarperCollins Christian Publishing, Inc. Translated into English by Jeffrey Stevenson.

Cover design: Faceout Studio, Molly von Borstel

Cover image: Shutterstock

First printing 2024

Printed in the United States of America

Trade paperback ISBN: 978-1-4335-9109-9
ePub ISBN: 978-1-4335-9111-2
PDF ISBN: 978-1-4335-9110-5

Library of Congress Cataloging-in-Publication Data

Names: Ávila, Ana, 1992-author.
Title: Make the most of your productivity : a guide to honoring God with your time / Ana Ávila.
Description: Wheaton, Illinois : Crossway, 2024. | Includes bibliographical references and index.
Identifiers: LCCN 2023024212 (print) | LCCN 2023024213 (ebook) | ISBN 9781433591099 (trade paperback) | ISBN 9781433591105 (pdf) | ISBN 9781433591112 (epub)
Subjects: LCSH: Productivity accounting. | Women—Economic conditions. | Christian women.
Classification: LCC HF5686.P86 A74 2024 (print) | LCC HF5686.P86 (ebook) | DDC 657.082—dc23/eng/20230919
LC record available at https://lccn.loc.gov/2023024212
LC ebook record available at https://lccn.loc.gov/2023024213

Crossway is a publishing ministry of Good News Publishers.

VP   33   32   31   30   29   28   27   26   25   24
15   14   13   12   11   10   9   8   7   6   5   4   3   2   1

For Uriel

Contents

PART 1

———————

FOUNDATIONS

1

A Call for Everyone

*Whether you eat or drink, or whatever
you do, do all to the glory of God.*

1 CORINTHIANS 10:31

MY QUARTER-LIFE CRISIS came a little earlier than expected.
I was twenty-three years old and sure of one thing: I was a failure.
Staring at the ceiling of my room with tears in my eyes, I thought
of all those people who at my age had already changed the world.
Blaise Pascal invented the mechanical calculator at the age of
nineteen. Mozart composed his first piece of music at the age of
five. After teaching herself with her grandfather's books, Sor Juana
Inés de la Cruz was already recognized for her philosophy in her
adolescence. What about me? What did I have to show that my
more than two decades on the planet had not been anything but
a waste of time and space? Absolutely nothing.

Maybe you can relate to the feeling: You work all the time, but
you feel like you never accomplish anything. You haven't won the

Nobel Prize. Your bank account is a little embarrassing. You follow all the dating advice, but singleness does not want to let go of you.

Or maybe you find yourself at the other extreme. You have never given much thought to achieving great things. You face life as it comes. Plans are not your thing. You suddenly look around and wonder, "How did I get here? Surely there must be more to life than just floating through it."

In this book we will discover that yes, there is much more for us than just floating through life. But we will also discover that this something else is very different from what we usually expect. Our lives are not valuable because of all the things we accomplish; our lives are valuable because of all the things God has accomplished on our behalf. Once we understand that, we are free to be truly productive.

What Is Productivity?

In his formidable satire *The Screwtape Letters*, C. S. Lewis warns us that "there are two equal and opposite errors into which our race can fall about the devils. One is to disbelieve in their existence. The other is to believe, and to feel an excessive and unhealthy interest in them."[1] These kinds of errors—equal and opposite ones—are our favorites as human beings in virtually every aspect of life, including productivity.

During my quarter-life crisis, I fell into one of two extremes. I thought I was not being productive (or that my productivity was useless) because I was not accomplishing "great things." I would set a goal, convinced that by reaching it I would become the

---

1   C. S. Lewis, *The Screwtape Letters: With Screwtape Proposes a Toast* (New York: HarperCollins, 2001), ix.

person I had always dreamed of being. But one of two outcomes always came about. Either I didn't reach my goal and crumbled, or I reached it and realized that it wasn't enough—I had to achieve even more.

At the other extreme are those who think productivity is irrelevant. They think that their life belongs to them and therefore they can do whatever they want, whenever they want, without anyone criticizing them for doing so. They deal with what comes up when it comes up—and if they don't want to deal with something, they just don't, and that's the end of the story.

The main problem is that we have an erroneous idea of what it means to be productive. Productivity is a concept that has its origins in the economic sciences and refers to a system's efficiency of production. It has to do with the relationship between the quantity of products that are made and the quantity of resources invested in producing them. In using this word to describe time management and organization, we have come to think that personal productivity simply means getting a lot done in a short amount of time.

We could try to eliminate the word "productivity," but we probably won't succeed, at least in the near future. For now, it will suffice to understand it differently. I like how Tim Challies defines the concept in his book *Do More Better*: "Productivity is effectively stewarding your gifts, talents, time, energy, and enthusiasm for the good of others and the glory of God."[2]

I would summarize it like this: the productive life is a life that seeks to honor God with all that you have. This means that

---

2   Tim Challies, *Do More Better: A Practical Guide to Productivity* (Minneapolis: Cruciform, 2015), 16.

productivity isn't just for big executives with seven meetings scheduled every day or for students overwhelmed by the typical college workload. A productive life applies to them and also to the housewife with three small children and unpredictable days, the retired grandfather who isn't quite sure what to do with his time, the nurse who works long shifts and lives one day at a time, and the janitor who has been cleaning the same building for fifteen years. Productivity is for everyone because we all have gifts, talents, time, energy, and enthusiasm. A productive person is someone who takes whatever resources they have (regardless of whether they are many or few, whether they are valued or overlooked) and seeks to use them to fulfill the purpose for which they were put on earth.

A cup is a good cup only to the extent that it fulfills the purpose for which it was designed: to hold liquid for drinking. We can say something similar about human beings. People live a good life, a productive life, only to the extent that they fulfill the purpose for which they were designed. This truth is intuitive for most people. Regardless of who they are and where they come from, at one time or another everyone has asked themselves, Why am I here? The most common question for children is, What do you want to be when you grow up? The idea that we are on earth for a good reason and that we have a purpose to fulfill is strongly rooted in the human heart. The problem arises when we don't know what that good reason is or how to discover our purpose. We wander through life leaning hopelessly toward one of two extremes of false productivity: working frantically for the wrong reasons or being passively carried along by circumstances.

This hunger for purpose isn't part of who we are by chance. The desire to know why we are here points to the fact that there is someone who can give us the answer. Like Mary Shelley's creature, we all desperately search for our maker. Fortunately, unlike Victor Frankenstein, the true Creator does not hide from us in disgust. He has revealed himself and revealed a lot about the reason he created us.

A Christian Perspective on Productivity

When we think of productivity from a Christian perspective, the first thing that might come to mind is the book of Proverbs. This book, which offers us wisdom, is full of warnings about laziness as well as exhortations to work diligently. And of course, reading Proverbs can give us many ideas on how to live a life that honors God by making good use of our time. However, it's a mistake to think that this is the only place in Scripture that provides wisdom regarding productivity. If we pay close attention, we will realize that the whole story of the Bible informs us about how we can live to honor the God who made us.

Created to Create

In the beginning, God created the heavens and the earth. (Gen. 1:1)

Why is there something instead of nothing? This is one of the most important questions that human beings have asked themselves since the beginning of history. Scripture reveals the answer in its first line: because in the beginning, God—a being that is outside of space and time, inconceivably free from the limitations of the laws of physics—spoke. And the world came into being.

In the beginning, God created everything. And he created everything good. He made a garden in which he placed two gardeners made in his image to tend it and to make it grow and prosper. He gave man and woman everything they needed to live in communion with him, to be satisfied as they fulfilled their purpose to create because they were made in the image of the Creator.

However, this was not enough for the gardeners. Even though they had work to do and everything they needed to do it well, they decided to direct their gaze toward the forbidden. They decided to question the Creator and, instead of tending to creation according to his will, they decided to use it as they pleased.

Adam and Eve ate of the forbidden fruit, and they turned their backs on God. Then, they died. They were expelled from the garden, the place they had been created to care for. What once would have been perfect joy would now require sweat, blood, and tears. Filling the land and making it flourish would not be easy, but it would still be their job.

We have followed their example. Every chance we have, we turn our backs on God. We shake our fist at heaven, challenging God and saying that our way of doing things is better. We do this not by eating forbidden fruits but by lying, coveting, envying—wasting our lives instead of living to reflect the character of the one who made us.

Although distorted by sin, the image that God placed in human beings is still in our hearts. Imperfectly and in an imperfect world, we create to show the world who the Creator is. When a lawyer defends the innocent, he is showing the justice of the one who defines what good is. When a mother coos to her child, she reflects the care of the perfect Father. When a janitor cleans a room, he shows that the God who designed the universe is a God of order. All work, paid or unpaid, public or private, is an opportunity to make the image of the one who created and sustains the world shine.

So we still have a mission. In fact, we have two.

Reached to Reach

Go therefore and make disciples of all nations. (Matt. 28:19)

God was not going to leave things as he found them in Genesis 3. He wants us back in close relationship with him. But how could a completely perfect God allow such impure beings as us back into his presence? Just as darkness cannot remain in light, so is our evil incompatible with the source of all that is good. The righteous one can't sweep sin under the rug and pretend it's not there.

There was only one solution. So God did the unthinkable: he took the form of a man and came to walk among us. He did it to show us what human beings look like when they perfectly reflect his image. Moreover, showing his perfect love and justice, Jesus died on a cross to take the blame that belonged to us. We would never have been able to pay off the sin debt that we owed to the Creator. He did it himself. Justice is fulfilled and darkness is dispelled from the hearts of those who repent of their wickedness and embrace what Jesus did on the cross as the only thing that can save them. Christ is the only one who can put us in right standing before God; he is the only one who can take us back to the Father.

Today we continue to fill the earth and make it flourish. However, as we work, we also proclaim the name of the one who gave himself on our behalf and taught us to walk in the truth, to walk in him. As we nurture the world that God has given us, we make disciples of all nations. God reached us in order that we might reach others. We were saved to save. That is our new mission. Every believer should live fulfilling this task, from the elderly woman interceding in secret, to the pastor preaching behind the pulpit. From the father reading the Bible to his little boy, to friends crying together over the pain of loss.

By the simple fact that we were reconciled to God, we can now tell the whole world to be reconciled to him. And we will walk in that mission until our Lord returns in glory and renews this sin-broken world, until he makes all things new and takes us home, where we will worship him for eternity.

Served to Serve

> Even the Son of Man came not to be served but to serve, and to give his life as a ransom for many. (Mark 10:45)

I don't know if it's because of our familiarity with the image of Jesus the carpenter in sandals, but we have lost our awe. We get excited about the idea of a celebrity liking one of our tweets and then go through the day without thinking even for a moment that the God of the universe, the Supreme Being, the one who is eternally blissful in himself, the one who needs nothing and no one, the one who created the stars and put the planets in their place, became man. He came to our home. And he didn't come to our home to claim honor (although he might well have done so). He came to our home to serve.

When we think of being productive, serving is perhaps the last thing on our minds. We want to be productive in order to reach the top of the corporate ladder. Maybe we want to be productive so that a lot of people will recognize our name or so that we have the money to buy that car we've always dreamed of. But that isn't what Jesus did. God left his glory to walk among us and offer himself on our behalf even unto death. He worked diligently for decades under the authority of a man he himself created, in a small workshop, in a small town, in a small country, without anyone recognizing him. He invested his life working with twelve men who had little to offer—a group that included traitors, liars, unbelievers, cowards, and a couple of brothers who thought they were worthy to sit next to the sovereign Lord of glory.

However, Jesus quickly demolished their dreams. He explained that in his kingdom, things work the other way around. The great serve. The first are slaves of all. Truly productive people are servants.

Just as God showed us his creative nature and invited us to create—just as he showed us his saving character and invites us to be part of his plan to save—so does he reveal his servant heart and call us to serve. We serve when we prepare a meal for our family. We serve when, however exhausting the week has been, we help our neighbor move. We serve when we invest our time teaching a child who is struggling with math. The needs around us never end. We Christians are called to recognize needs, extend our hands, and reflect the character of the God who cares for his own with love and humility.

This is the story of a creator, savior, and servant God. It's the gospel story. It's the story he invites us to be a part of, seeking to make the most of everything we have to reflect his glory.

The Gospel Transforms Our Productivity

To be productive is to embrace the reality of what God does in us and to respond in worship through our work and our rest.

What God Does

Christianity does not teach that we must do many things to be at peace with God. On the contrary, we do things because, through Jesus's sacrifice, we are already at peace with God. The verdict is in. With this confidence we can seek to have a productive life, knowing that even if we fail miserably, there is grace from God to keep us going. Matt Perman summed it up this way: "The only way to be productive is to realize that you don't have to be."[3] Truly productive people do not seek to be productive in order to discover their purpose but is productive because they have already found their purpose in God and now want to live it out.

This will change the way we view our successes and failures. Victories don't make me feel superior because I know that separated from God, I am nothing. Defeats don't make

---

3 Matt Perman, *What's Best Next: How the Gospel Transforms the Way You Get Things Done* (Grand Rapids: Zondervan, 2014), 104.

me hopeless because I know that my value is in Jesus and not in my performance.

What I Do

God is God and does not need us, but he still delights in making us part of his plan. He uses our efforts to accomplish his purposes. Since creation, he has called us to work. Although he could have made a world where produce would sprout without effort, he called us to till the soil. And at the same time, Jesus taught us to rest in the fact that the Father feeds the birds of the air and will feed us too. Productivity is a paradox—it's work and it's rest.

This fact will change the way I look at my day-to-day activities. I can work hard knowing that God uses my every effort. I can rest easy knowing that the final outcome is in the Lord's hands.

It's impossible to remain in this centered view of productivity all the time. We are very prone to wander. Some of us tend to work tirelessly to prove our worth. Others fall into laziness and allow themselves to be carried along by the flow of everyday life events. Far from remaining focused on the identity that the gospel offers us, many of us feel on top of the world when things are going well and feel like the worst garbage on earth when everything seems to be going wrong. Figure 1 illustrates how true productivity is found in having good rhythms of work and rest (by neither working all the time nor resting all the time) and a gospel-centered view of oneself (by neither considering ourselves the best nor the worst), with productivity maintaining a balance of work and rest, confidence and humility.

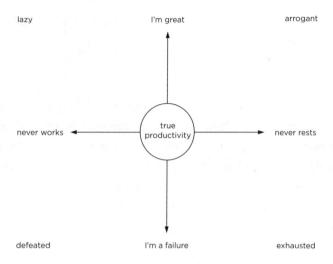

Figure 1. True productivity

Although it can be difficult to determine what quadrant we are in, it can be helpful to return regularly to this graph in order to evaluate how we are living out the mission God has given us. Are we fulfilling our responsibilities diligently? Are we resting assured that, at the end of the day, God is sovereign and uses our efforts as he wills? If we are successful, do we believe it's only because of our merits? If we fail, are we remembering that nothing can take away any spiritual blessing that has been given to us in Jesus?

Being productive doesn't mean doing many things in a short period of time. It does not mean working every minute of the day. Rather, it is seeking to honor God with what you have, making an effort when it's time to make an effort and resting when it's time to rest.

The productive life is a life centered on the truth that God uses and sustains us. But above all, it's a life centered on the identity that the gospel of God offers us. We are productive not because we have to be but because we are privileged to be part of the mission of God, who is renewing all things in Christ Jesus.

For Reflection

1. What were your thoughts on productivity before reading this chapter? How has your perspective changed?

2. Which quadrant of productivity are you currently in (see figure 1)? What part of the gospel story must you continually remind yourself of in order to get closer to the center of true productivity?

3. How would your life change if you always sought to get closer to the center of true productivity?

Action Points

Start reflecting on the concept of productivity in your devotional life. When you read the Bible, ask yourself, How does applying this passage lead me to honor God more where I am and with what I have? When you pray, ask for wisdom to do even the simplest things for the glory of God (1 Cor. 10:31).

2

For the Love of God and Others

*You shall love the Lord your God with all your heart
and with all your soul and with all your mind. This is
the great and first commandment. And a second is like
it: You shall love your neighbor as yourself. On these two
commandments depend all the Law and the Prophets.*

MATTHEW 22:37–40

LOOKING BACK, I am not surprised that I was completely disappointed in myself during my quarter-life crisis. An echo rang in my head that had been with me since I was a little girl: *You can achieve great things. You will change the world!* That voice both drove me and terrified me. It would show me everything I could achieve and then humiliate me because I was so far from achieving it.

Many of us know that voice well. For some, the words have changed: *You could have achieved great things. You could have changed the world. But just look at yourself!* Our life is so different from what we expected it would be that we have stopped trying. Whatever happens, what difference does it make?

That inner voice isn't completely wrong. It's true that we can achieve great things and change the world. Every human being has this capacity, from their birth to the day they die. The problem is how we define "great things" and "changing the world." Usually these phrases make us think in terms of economic wealth, fame, academic degrees, or international travel. Few people will admit that this is their concept of greatness, but our daily lives reveal it. We pursue material rewards or social recognition and get depressed when we don't get them. We look at our neighbor with envy because he travels to countries we didn't even know existed, because his house is bigger, or because his children attend more expensive schools.

This hunger for greatness is natural. The problem is that we are looking to satisfy it in the wrong places. Augustine of Hippo, who converted to Christianity after years of debauchery, recognized this truth when he said in his *Confessions*, "You have made us for yourself, O Lord, and our heart is restless until it rests in you."[1] We are prone to jump from one thing to another (achievements or pleasures) hoping that something will make us feel that we finally possess what we have so longed for. But if, as the Westminster Shorter Catechism says, "the chief end of man" is "to glorify God, and to enjoy him forever," it's not surprising that nothing we acquire and none of our achievements satisfy us for more than an instant.[2] If the emptiness in our hearts is the size of eternity, there is only one person who can fill it (Eccl. 3:11).

1　Augustine of Hippo, *Confessions*, bk. 1, chap. 1.
2　Westminster Shorter Catechism, Q. 1, A. 1.

This is good news. To satisfy our hunger for greatness we do not have to make a certain amount of money, earn three university degrees, travel the world, or live in a house with a big yard and a swimming pool. To satisfy our hunger for greatness we don't have to wait to get all our to-dos in order, develop excellent reading and exercise habits, or keep our email inbox at zero. To satisfy our hunger for greatness we need only look to the one who made us and let him nourish and guide us. When we do, a curious thing happens: we realize that we have been using productivity backward, as a means of obtaining what we need instead of a means of offering to others what God has already given us.

One of the biggest mistakes you can make in trying to become a productive person is to think that your productivity is for you. It's true that organizing your work-related resources the night before will make your mornings less chaotic. Yes, designing a meal plan will save you time and money at the grocery store. Learning to choose your priorities will surely make it possible for you to carry out many projects that previously only existed in your head. The personal benefits of productivity are undeniable, but they are also secondary in importance.

This is because, overall, productivity isn't about achieving; it's about loving. Productivity is the way we seek to put into action the two great commandments that summarize the whole of God's law. Matthew 22:36–40 records Jesus's explanation of this:

> Teacher, which is the great commandment in the Law? And he said to him, "You shall love the Lord your God with all your heart and with all your soul and with all your mind. This is the great and first commandment. And a second is like it: You shall

love your neighbor as yourself. On these two commandments depend all the Law and the Prophets." (Matt. 22:36–40)

In these four verses, Jesus shows us what true greatness is. This is the way you and I can change the world: by loving God and loving others. Love must be the reason for our productivity. We can't base it on money or the satisfaction of finishing a to-do list or even peace of mind, although all of these may be the result as well. True productivity comes from taking our eyes off ourselves and pouring out our lives for the glory of God and the good of others. After all, that was Jesus's example: "Greater love has no one than this, that someone lay down his life for his friends" (John 15:13). My productivity isn't for myself but to show my neighbor who God is as I serve that neighbor.

This, of course, doesn't mean that our own lives are worthless. It doesn't mean that our needs are not important. On the contrary, it means that the God of the universe takes care of us while using us to take care of others. In the Bible we find reminders to take care of our bodies and to rest, but Scripture also calls us to focus on the kingdom of God by trusting him to take care of us (Matt. 6:25–34).

We can't expect all this to be easy. After all, the most productive person in the world died unjustly on a cross. That is the pattern we see throughout Scripture: since the fall in the garden of Eden, work has a cost. Obedience hurts. There are "thorns and thistles" (Gen. 3:18); there is injustice. There is fatigue, there is suffering, there is ingratitude. The book of Proverbs shows us how things should be when it says, "The soul of the diligent is richly supplied" (Prov. 13:4). However, Ecclesiastes offers us the bitter pill of reality in a world like ours: "What does man gain by all the toil at which he toils under the sun?" (Eccl. 1:3).

It's essential to remember the reality of the fall as we seek to honor God with all that we have. Using our time well is no guarantee that we will have a long and fulfilling life. Managing our energy efficiently does not ensure that we will never get sick. Being wise with our finances does not mean that we will amass great wealth. The Bible is full of men and women who honored God. Some were rich and some were poor. Some were widely recognized and some were despised. Some saw their grandchildren and great-grandchildren, while others died in their youth. Hundreds of productive lives, very different from one another, but with one thing in common: loving God and others from where they were and with what they had.

If we have our sights set on money, health, or recognition, we will undoubtedly be disappointed. God never promises to give us any of these things on this earth, even if we live each moment seeking to honor him with what we have. Rather, the promise is that when we fix our eyes on his kingdom, he will give us what we need to live (Matt. 6:33). From that point on, we do not know what our lot will be. While we may see glimpses of his blessings here on earth, the real reward is found in eternity.

Far from discouraging us, this should take a great weight off our shoulders. We are free to be productive not in order to get but in order to give, not to reach a certain standard but to reach others with our service. This is, as Tim Keller wrote, "the blessed rest that only self-forgetfulness brings."[3] I have received so much

---

3   Timothy Keller, *The Freedom of Self-Forgetfulness: The Path to True Christian Joy* (Chorley, UK: 10Publishing, 2012), 43.

from the Lord that my heart overflows with love. I can show that love by using my time, energy, skills, attention, and any other resources to meet the needs of those around me and show them the God in whom I delight.

Some of us don't even bother with the issue of productivity because we feel we have nothing to offer. Maybe you're a mom with three young children, taking one day at a time. Maybe you have lived for years with a chronic illness that prevents you from doing much more than getting out of bed. It may be that the only thing on your mind right now is raising your family in the midst of a major economic crisis.

I won't pretend that I understand how difficult your situation is. However, I would like to encourage you to look at things from another perspective. Each of us has something to offer. We find this truth in one of Jesus's parables:

> For it will be like a man going on a journey, who called his servants and entrusted to them his property. To one he gave five talents, to another two, to another one, to each according to his ability. Then he went away. He who had received the five talents went at once and traded with them, and he made five talents more. So also he who had the two talents made two talents more. But he who had received the one talent went and dug in the ground and hid his master's money. Now after a long time the master of those servants came and settled accounts with them. And he who had received the five talents came forward, bringing five talents more, saying, "Master, you delivered to me five talents; here, I have made five talents more." His master said to him, "Well done, good and faithful

the end and the result will be something that benefits others. I don't know where Van Booy puts his faith as he writes, but I am convinced that God is the only place safe enough to put mine. If I rest on how diligent or smart I am, I'll fall apart when a bad day comes along. However, no matter how I feel, I can rest assured that God is always omniscient and omnipotent. I can keep walking, even if my steps are small and seemingly useless; God carries me to the end.

When fears come and we are confronted with our own inability, we can say, "Yes, it's true that I don't know everything. It's true that I have many limitations. But I'm here for a reason." As Christians, we can rest in the sovereignty of the God who sends and empowers us. We can face whatever comes our way knowing that the outcome does not depend on us. A person of faith can work hard and also rest in the fact that God uses their limited efforts for his glory.

Purpose

It's no use running if we are going in the wrong direction. As consultant Peter Drucker wrote, "There is surely nothing quite so useless as doing with great efficiency what should not be done at all."[3] Identifying where we are going is essential. Unfortunately, it's difficult for many to know for sure what they should be doing. Today we have more options than ever and, instead of this allowing us to make great strides, it overwhelms us. A few centuries ago, if your parents were shoemakers, you would be a shoemaker too. Today, the options are endless.

There are many things we could be doing. Lots of professional and educational opportunities, lots of needs to fill, lots of books

3   Peter F. Drucker, "Managing for Business Effectiveness," *Harvard Business Review*, May 1963.

to read, lots of emails to answer, lots of meetings to attend. How can we not feel overwhelmed? A productive person understands that their resources are limited and that they cannot do everything they could be doing. A productive person takes the time to identify where they should invest their energy, attention, and skills. A productive person says no to everything else, respectfully but firmly.

Identifying what you should be doing isn't easy, nor is it an exact science. It's not something you'll do once and that's it. Rather, being a person of purpose means continually meditating on the direction you're heading in and how your activities are leading you there, both on a large scale ("Should I take this job?") as well as on a small scale ("Do I really have to read this report today?"). While all of this may sound overwhelming, we need not be alarmed. We don't have a sadistic god who enjoys seeing us stuck in the dead ends of life as if we were mice in a labyrinth. We have the God of the Bible and his commandments. As long as we stay within these, we are free to make prudent and safe decisions. As Kevin DeYoung writes,

> God is not a magic 8-ball we shake up and peer into whenever we have a decision to make. He is a good God who gives us brains, shows us the way of obedience, and invites us to take risks for Him. We know God has a plan for our lives. That's wonderful. The problem is we think He's going to tell us the wonderful plan before it unfolds.[4]

Being a person of purpose does not mean waiting for an angel to come down from heaven to reveal to you whether you should

4 Kevin DeYoung, *Just Do Something: A Liberating Approach to Finding God's Will* (Chicago: Moody, 2009), 26.

study chemistry or theater. Being a person of purpose means seeking wisdom through the resources available to you (such as the Bible, common sense, and the people around you) and making a decision trusting that, in the end, God will accomplish his perfect purposes using our imperfect efforts.

Diligence

Being diligent does not mean working all the time but rather doing what needs to be done (including resting) no matter how we feel. It's striving to do what you have to do and leaving the rest in the Lord's hands.

Emotions are important, but we cannot unquestioningly rely on them. Sometimes our body will ask for rest but our emotions will say that we can't allow ourselves to rest because if we do, we will fail. At other times we'll be ready to work on a project that we committed to deliver that same day but our emotions will tell us to relax for a while, watching videos and having a cup of coffee. The idea of following your heart is appealing; yet, what happens when all your heart wants is to watch another season of your favorite series in one sitting?

We can't control whether we feel like doing something, but we can control how we respond to that feeling. Lack of motivation isn't lack of ability. Even if I don't feel like doing laundry, I am still able to do laundry. Even if I don't feel like writing, I am still able to write. There are few things as liberating as discovering that we are not slaves to our emotions. We can recognize and accept them and still do the opposite of what they ask of us. The difference between productive and unproductive people isn't what they feel but how they respond to feelings.

Depth

Faith gives us reasons to be productive. Purpose tells us what we should do. Diligence helps us get started. And when we let go of superficiality and seek to go deeper into a task, it helps us finish.

In our hyperconnected world, our attention is pulled in hundreds of directions all the time. We have lost the ability to concentrate and focus on what is most important. Few of us can sit down and finish what we started without being interrupted by trivialities over and over again. I remember my first months as a work-from-home mom: While my baby cried in my arms for extended periods of time because he couldn't sleep, my frustration mounted by the second because I had an overdue project I needed to work on. As I worked on my project, my mind wandered to the messy kitchen I had to tidy up. As I tidied up the kitchen, I worried because I hadn't finished the homework for my weekly study group. While I was in the weekly study group, the clock ticking loudly in my head and reminding me that I was supposed to meet a girl from church for coffee, I couldn't get my attention to stay focused and delve undistractedly into the task before me. There was always something else to do, and I felt I had to do it right then and there.

The to-do list never ends. There will always be a new email to read, a new load of laundry to do, a new meeting to attend, a new essay to write, a new sermon to prepare, a new patient to see, or a new person to counsel. And, of course, the distractions are also endless. When we say yes to something, we say no to everything else. Some noes are temporary (while we are working, we say no to social media, but we can check it in the afternoon). Other noes are permanent (we turn down an invitation to a meeting to which we have little to contribute). Depth leads us to embrace what is most important and let go of the rest. Superficiality leads us to want to hold on to everything at the same time. Depth implies that when we say yes to something, we focus on it and do it to the best of our ability. Superficiality causes us to be dragged here and there by distractions and worries; we do things, but we do not do them well.

Being in Order to Do; Doing in Order to Be

How do we cultivate these character traits? Theologian John M. Frame writes that "moral maturity comes by constant practice."[5] We are developing our character every time we make a decision in faith and not in unbelief, every time we walk with purpose instead of simply wandering around, every time we are diligent instead of lazy, every time we stay deep instead of running toward distraction. No human being becomes a productive person overnight. We must stop waiting for some sort of magical and immediate change that will revolutionize our entire lives. There are no shortcuts. Interestingly, to be productive we need a mature character, but to cultivate that mature character we need to make productive decisions.

Productivity isn't a destination but rather a lifelong journey. Every step counts. God uses our ordinary decisions to transform us into what he designed us to be: people who honor him with everything they have.

Jesus Is Our Example and More Than Our Example

If we want to see a perfectly productive life in action, we need only turn to the first books of the New Testament. Jesus continually

5   John M. Frame, *Nature's Case for God: A Brief Biblical Argument* (Bellingham, WA: Lexham, 2018), 75.

demonstrated that he was a person of faith, purpose, diligence, and depth. We see each of these in Scripture:

- Faith: "I came from God and I am here. I came not of my own accord, but he sent me" (John 8:42)
- Purpose: "Truly, truly, I say to you, the Son can do nothing of his own accord, but only what he sees the Father doing. For whatever the Father does, that the Son does likewise" (John 5:19)
- Diligence: "My Father is working until now, and I am working" (John 5:17)
- Depth: "Seek first the kingdom of God and his righteousness, and all these things will be added to you. Therefore do not be anxious about tomorrow, for tomorrow will be anxious for itself. Sufficient for the day is its own trouble" (Matt. 6:33–34)

Without a doubt, Jesus's life does not resemble what many have in mind when they think of productivity. He was not running around at full speed but rather spent his time eating with his friends and withdrawing himself to pray. He did not heal all the sick, nor did he visit all the cities. He did not use his influence to gain a fortune or to climb to a certain social position. Jesus was productive in looking to the Father and living out the mission he had given him, working when it was time to work and resting when it was time to rest.

However, the hope that Christians have is that Jesus is much more than our example. Yes, by looking at him we can discover what a truly productive life looks like. But we are also confronted with how far we are from having a character like his. If Jesus were only our example, we would soon fall into despair. The standard is too high. Thus, the gospel is good news for a good reason. Jesus walked the earth not only to show us how we should live; he also came to die and pay for all the times we have not lived as we should. His perfection is now counted as ours: "For our sake he made him to be sin who knew no sin, so that in him we might become the righteousness of God" (2 Cor. 5:21). We rest in this truth as we strive to walk one step at a time in the right direction, trusting God to transform us as we "behold the glory" of Jesus (2 Cor. 3:18).

For Reflection

1. What are the three biggest obstacles to your productivity? What character quality do you need to develop to overcome them?

2. Think of an unproductive moment you had last week. Is there a story from the life of Jesus that shows you the way you should have acted? How does the gospel of Jesus give you hope to keep going even though you have failed?

Action Points

Choose a character trait you want to cultivate and write down three simple actions you can continuously put into practice in order to develop it. For example, to cultivate depth, you could turn off your cell phone when having dinner with your family, or to cultivate faith, you could memorize a passage from the Bible, such as Romans 8:34.

PART 2

PRINCIPLES

4

Time

You have time to do what you should be doing.

LIFE DOES NOT HAVE A PAUSE BUTTON. The clock does not stop. Seconds run by without asking our permission, and we rarely stop to think about what that means. When we do, we can feel terrible anguish. The minutes slip away from us like water seeping into a boat as we try to put things in order. We desperately try to cover the cracks with our hands until we give up and simply let the weight of the ocean sink us.

It doesn't have to be this way. Christians can look at the unceasing passage of time with hope. Despite our personal defeats and the failures of humankind, history continues to move toward the moment when evil will finally be defeated, when there will be no more weeping, no more pain, no more death, no more anxiety, no more stress. Contemplating that glorious day transforms the way we see the moment we are living in today.

In the midst of the ups and downs of life we can work hard, using everything we have to the best of our ability to fulfill the two greatest commandments and the Great Commission that the Lord has given us. We offer our time, skills, energy, and attention to love God and others while making disciples by preaching the gospel to those around us. During these ups and downs of life we can rest, knowing that the victory has already been given in Christ Jesus. Our defeats do not change the verdict. There is grace to keep going when we stumble.

Our God is a God who knows that we are dust and yet delights to use us for his glory. Knowing even better than we do the laziness or eagerness in our hearts, he is pleased to make us part of his plan. The Bible teaches us that before the foundation of the world, God prepared good works for us to walk in (Eph. 2:10). We do not have all the details about what kind of tasks the Lord will lead us to perform during the rest of our lives, but we do not need the details. God guides us one step at a time through his word, the church, and the Holy Spirit. He will not allow us to go astray. Our God is a sovereign God who, in one way or another, uses all our imperfect efforts to fulfill his perfect purposes, carrying us in the belly of a great fish if necessary (Jonah 2:10).

Overall, being aware of this divine sovereignty brings peace. If the Lord of time and space has placed us here and prepared works for us a very long time ago, we can rest easy. We have everything we need to walk in obedience. We have time to do the things we should be doing according to the purpose God has for each of us.

The Way to the Heart of True Productivity

God is the one most interested in you and me using our time well. He isn't looking down from heaven waiting for us to throw our lives away in order to punish us. On the contrary, he began the good work in us and he will finish it (Phil. 1:6). If we want wisdom to be productive—to live a life that honors him with all we have—we need only ask in faith. This is a prayer that God promises to answer (James 1:5–7).

Of course, asking for wisdom is just the beginning. We need to know the word of God and walk in obedience, trusting that the Lord will make our steps straight as we do so. In the process, how can we start making better use of our time? Here are some ideas:

1. Think about time. Thinking about the passage of time can be overwhelming. Many of us can't stand listening to the sound of a clock ticking away the seconds that will never return. But facing reality is the first step toward living with wisdom. The psalmist recognized that being aware of the brevity of life is important for living in a way that pleases the Lord: "Teach us to number our days that we may get a heart of wisdom" (Ps. 90:12).

Visual reminders of this can be helpful. I have an hourglass on my desk that I use for my deep work sessions.[1] For me, it demonstrates the importance of making the most of every moment. But it's not an accusatory reminder. It definitely motivates me to strive to use every minute to the best of my ability, but it also makes me thank God for redeeming even my clumsiest efforts. Time marches on and his plans will be fulfilled. I am privileged to be part of them.

2. Value your time. If all lives are equally valuable and all lives are lived in time, every minute of your life has exactly the same

---

1 According to Cal Newport, deep work is "the act of focusing without distraction on a cognitively demanding task." Cal Newport, "Deep Work: Rules for Focused Success in a Distracted World," November 20, 2015, https://calnewport.com/.

value as a minute of your neighbor's life. It doesn't matter if your neighbor is a top executive or a celebrity who has a personal assistant. It doesn't matter if your neighbor spends the day taking an elevator up and down a building for work meetings while you're at home taking care of your kids or running a small business. To use our time well, we must learn to value it.

In his book *Spiritual Disciplines for the Christian Life*, Donald Whitney wrote that "if people threw away their money as thoughtlessly as they throw away their time, we would think them insane."[2] One of the easiest ways to value your time is to be aware of what you're spending it on. Take some time midmorning and before bedtime to reflect on what you have done with your hours throughout the day and readjust your strategy if necessary.

3. Learn from the example of others. Who do you admire? Observe how that person uses their time. The Bible is the perfect place to start because in the Gospels we find the most productive person in history in the flesh. Jesus lived every second for the glory of God and the good of others, thereby challenging all our preconceived ideas about productivity. He did not hurry or stress out but spent much time eating with his friends, playing with children, and praying in the wilderness. Jesus did not accumulate goods and did not mind letting many of his followers go. He did not heal all the sick nor did he travel to all places. Instead, he took on human limits and fulfilled his mission within those limits.

In the Scriptures we also meet Moses, Joshua, David, Esther, Ruth, Mary, Paul, and many, many more. Some were prophets and others rulers; several were recognized and others were rejected;

2   Donald S. Whitney, *Spiritual Disciplines for the Christian Life* (Colorado Springs: NavPress, 2014), 167.

some were educated and others came from very humble families. However, each of them can show us a little of what it's like to seek to please the Lord in the situation where he has placed us.

Another valuable resource is the biographies of people who have had a positive influence on the world. Of course, just because someone is famous doesn't mean they were productive (and just because someone has gone unnoticed doesn't mean they weren't). Yet, the most useful thing about good biographies isn't that they share curious facts about a person's life but that they look closely at the trajectory of a person's life. As we learn more stories of men and women who have transformed their environment, we will realize that productive people come in all shapes and sizes, but they also have similar characteristics, such as humility, a hunger to learn, determination, perseverance, and more.

Finally, we have the example of the people around us, live and in full color. Observe how people who are close to you spend their minutes and initiate friendly conversations about this topic when you have the opportunity. Your desire is to learn, so ask more questions than you make statements. And pay special attention to the elderly. They have experience and much wisdom to offer us, the fruit both of their own victories as well as their failures.

4. Plan with time in mind. Planning is good and necessary; Scripture warns us about the right way to do it: "The plans of the heart belong to man, but the answer of the tongue is from the Lord. All the ways of a man are pure in his own eyes, but the Lord weighs the spirit. Commit your work to the Lord, and your plans will be established" (Prov. 16:1–3). Thus, we plan and at the same time we depend on God. Recognizing that God establishes our paths does not mean that we can sit back and wait for things to happen; that would be to ignore the clear commands of Scripture to work hard. Putting our works in the hands of the Lord means that we make an effort and surrender all our efforts to him. Ultimately, we want the will of him who is infinitely wise to be done. If he allows plans to change, we do not lose heart or become bitter because we know that this too will work for our good (Rom. 8:28). But if we don't plan in the first place, we end up wasting the resources that the Lord has given us to manage. As we learn from the parable of the talents, hiding on earth what God has given us isn't an option. We have to go and do business with what he has entrusted to us.

Yet, making plans isn't enough; to be productive you have to make good plans. Many of us like to make lists to organize our to-dos and feel a little more prepared to face the day with diligence when we do. The problem is that we tend to forget that every task we perform takes time. We say, "I'll do this tomorrow," but we don't think through all the details; we end up juggling mile-long to-do lists instead of being realistic and realizing that we only have twenty-four hours in a day and that these hours are enough to do the things we should be doing. Being aware of how much time each of our responsibilities takes is the first step in identifying what is too much in our schedules and starting to say no more often.

When you make plans, make plans with time in mind. Have a clear idea of how much time you will need for each task you want to perform, and start to set limits on what you will do and when you will do it. Planning with time in mind is difficult at first—we tend to be overly optimistic about how much time we will need to complete a task—but with practice it becomes more and more natural. Checking your to-do list against your calendar will help you be more realistic and only commit to the things you can actually do. You may be discouraged when you realize there are many things you will need to give up. It's common to think big and imagine that we can do a lot of things on any given day. And if we don't remember that we are humans and not robots, our plans will fall apart. There's time for every matter.

If Only

"If only." These words are dangerous. They are the words we take refuge in to avoid doing what we know we should be doing. They are the words that make us look longingly at an imaginary world in which things are just a *little* different, while time slips through our fingers. In that imaginary world, a single detail seems to change the entire course of our lives.

"If only my son would sleep better, I could read the Bible more often." "If only I didn't have to work on the Internet, I wouldn't waste so much time on social media." "If only I had the money to go to the gym, I would start exercising."

Staying in the realm of "if only" is very tempting. Life is full of things we know we should be doing. I do not need to convince any Christian of the importance of obeying the commandments of Scripture: reading the Bible, praying, fasting, worshiping with other Christians, caring for the needy, discipling, and preaching the gospel. Add to that our family responsibilities, our work, and our basic needs—such as eating and sleeping—and it's no wonder we feel we have no time to do anything at all.

But "if only" isn't the solution. In fact, all it does is help us hide the problem. It numbs our consciences instead of allowing us to be confronted by our sin of spiritual apathy or laziness. It makes us victims of our circumstances instead of leading us to ask for wisdom to change things.

What sets us free is understanding that we have the time to do what we should be doing. We can obey the commands of Scripture and fulfill the responsibilities God has entrusted to us. This may mean that we have to give up commitments that we made without considering the time they would take, time that would be better spent on our family or ministry. We probably also need to change our expectations of what our obedience should look like. In our current circumstances, we may not be able to have a picture-perfect devotional life, but that does not mean that we can't feed on the word at all. Our work may not allow us to completely eliminate social media, but that doesn't mean we can't limit our use of it. Maybe our budget doesn't allow us to go to the gym, but that doesn't mean we can't exercise at home and try to eat healthier.

Overall, we don't need to live in a hurry or worry that we don't have enough hours in the day. Let's start from the reality that we have time to do the things we should be doing and then evaluate our lives in the light of Scripture to discover what things we should let go of and what things we should embrace. You may have to give up the extra income from a second job to spend more time with your family. Or maybe you should embrace a new ministry in your local church instead of spending so much time on social media.

Further, making good use of time isn't a onetime thing. The Christian's task is to seek wisdom from God continually, recognizing that "for everything there is a season, and a time for every matter under heaven" (Eccl. 3:1). Sometimes you have to let go and sometimes you have to embrace. At times we will need to focus on rest while at other times we will need to work extra hard. Discerning how to use the minutes we have will not always be easy, but we can rest assured that the Lord of time holds us in his hands and redeems our efforts.

For Reflection

1. How do you feel when you think about the passage of time?

2. Think of a person you admire and know well. How do they spend their time? If you have the chance to do so, ask them directly about this.

3. How has living in the "if only" limited your productivity?

Action Points

Make a list of all the things you want to do tomorrow. Above each item, write down how long it will take you to complete it (be realistic). Download the daily planner that you can find on my webpage at http://anaavila.org/24hours and arrange the tasks on your list according to the time each one will take. Then add your daily activities—such as sleeping, eating, commuting, getting ready to leave home, spending time with your family, and so on—to the daily planner. Was twenty-four hours enough? Do you have more or less time than you expected? What changes can you implement to make the most of tomorrow?

5

Limits

Bad news: you can't do it all.

I LIKE TO THINK that I can achieve anything. That nothing is beyond my reach. That if I try hard enough, I can understand everything. That if I organize my unfinished tasks better, I can read a couple hundred books a year. That sleep isn't as necessary as the seven projects I committed myself to all at the same time. That exercise will not make any difference in my medical test results. That fruits and vegetables are just a suggestion. That if I answer that email first thing in the morning, my boss will see how responsible I am. That if I say the right words, my friend will finally understand that she must take responsibility for her actions. That if I only read the Bible and pray only once in a while, I'll still have an intimate relationship with God.

In short, I like to think I have no limits. Although my energy plummets at six o'clock in the evening, I prefer to convince myself that I will write "in a little while" and that right now I can watch some TV. Even though I know my family has a history of diabetes, I prefer to convince myself that it's okay if I eat another piece of cake. Although I know I need to remember the gospel every day, I prefer to convince myself that it's okay if I put off my Bible reading until tomorrow (again). Although my schedule already has enough commitments, I prefer to convince myself that I will be able to fulfill the responsibilities of a new ministry at church. I like to think that limits are in my head and that if I try hard enough, I can overcome them and achieve anything I set my mind to.

However, the reality is that limits are not in my head but in my nature. The temptation to be free of all limits has pursued us since Eden. The serpent whispered, "Eat [this] . . . and you will be like God" (Gen. 3:5). The first humans fell into the trap. Adam and Eve were created in the image of God, but that was not enough for them. They were limited. They were creatures who needed the Creator in order to exist and be sustained. They had to eat and rest, and they depended on God's revelation to know what was good and what was bad. So they listened to the voice that told them there was a way to escape their humanity and become equal to God. Yet, far from freeing them from their limits, sin increased those restrictions with greater force: to their natural condition as creatures would be added pain, sweat, and sickness.

Today we do not eat forbidden fruits, but we continue to run away from what makes us recognize that we are dependent and vulnerable. Some seek to escape their human limitations by working frantically: reading every new self-help book, taking crash courses and food supplements, or trying to adopt a polyphasic sleep schedule.[1] Others take the opposite route: they try to escape their limitations by simply ignoring them. Although they know that the average person needs between seven and nine hours of sleep, they claim they are the exception. They don't go to the doctor or worry about their diet or exercise. They say yes to every interesting project that comes their way, thinking they'll figure out how to deliver everything on time later.

However, true productivity isn't achieved by fooling yourself. The first step to stop being a slave to limits is to recognize that you have them. This reality confronts me every time I sit down to work. I start the day with the assurance that I will be able to write about five thousand words before I go to bed. But even though I carefully organize my work time and eliminate virtually all distractions, I usually end up disappointed when I see the word count at the end of the afternoon. The next morning, instead of adjusting my expectations and being realistic about what I can do in a day's work, I wake up convinced that this time it will be different, that all I need to do is adjust my routine a bit and wake up a little earlier or maybe isolate myself from the world and write in a cabin in the woods.

I can't deny that there are times when I do need to be more diligent. There are days when I let myself be overcome by work or domestic difficulties and fall into a downward spiral of procrastination and unproductivity. I neither work nor rest; I just avoid my responsibilities. Yet, even on days when I am diligent and accomplish the things I know I must do, the lie that "you will be

---

1 Sleep in short segments over a twenty-four-hour period rather than in a single block of seven to nine hours.

like God" (Gen. 3:5) causes me to end my day feeling defeated. It's never enough. I want to do more. I want to be more.

The desire to be more indicates that our hearts have once again wandered in their quest for greatness. Instead of resting in the fact that it's God who sustains my family, I am convinced that everything will be okay only if I do the right things the right way. Instead of seeing my work as a service to others that reflects how God served me, I stop sleeping to deliver everything on time and impress my colleagues with my efficiency. When we reject our limits—whether by overworking or trying to pretend they do not exist—we are seeking greatness in ourselves rather than in God. We are seeking to demonstrate that we do not need help or a Helper.

However, none of us was created to carry the burden of the world on our shoulders. We were created to reflect the image of the one who effortlessly holds the universe in the palm of his hand. We do this not only through our work but also through our rest and our limitations. When a teacher declines an invitation to take on additional classes so that he can spend more time at home instead of trying to earn a little extra money at the expense of his family, he is proclaiming that only God can be fully present everywhere at once. When a writer refers a colleague for a job opportunity instead of pretending to have mastered the subject while spending sleepless nights doing research, she is recognizing that only God knows all the facts before the beginning of time. When a parent secretly prays for the salvation of his little one instead of offering candy for good behavior, he is pointing to the only one who can transform people from the depths of the heart. As Jen Wilkin writes in her book *None Like Him*, we are not called to be "like

God in his unlimited divinity, [but] we are to be like God in our limited humanity. We are capable of bearing his image as we were intended only when we embrace our limits."[2]

The psalmist reminds us that human beings are a paradox of greatness and smallness:

When I look at your heavens, the work of your fingers,
 the moon and the stars, which you have set in place,
what is man that you are mindful of him,
 and the son of man that you care for him?

Yet you have made him a little lower than the heavenly beings
 and crowned him with glory and honor:
You have given him dominion over the works of your hands;
 you have put all things under his feet. (Ps. 8:3–6)

To accept our limits is not to deny the incalculable value we have as human beings. It's true that God has granted each one of us an enormous potential that can be used for his glory and the good of others. But it's also true that we are small and fragile.

To embrace our limits is to recognize that God is the only one who can remedy all things. He makes us part of his plan and—like the servants in the parable of the talents—we must work with excellence and fulfill what he has commanded us to do with diligence. However, every effort must be founded on the conviction that God alone is omnipotent, omniscient, and omnipresent, the only one who controls all things and in whom our future rests.

2 Jen Wilkin, *None Like Him: 10 Ways God is Different from Us (and Why That's a Good Thing)* (Wheaton, IL: Crossway, 2016), 25.

If God is the only omnipotent one, I can rest every night even if I feel that my responsibilities are too much for me. If God is the only omniscient one, I can consult other people without fear of being called ignorant. If God is the only omnipresent one, I can enjoy playtime with my family without feeling guilty about being away from work.

God made us as creatures who need to sleep, eat, and drink for a good reason—to show us that the world does not depend on us. Every night's sleep is a reminder that we don't need to be working to keep the universe moving. Every time we sit down to eat it becomes a reminder that we exist not only to nourish but also to be nourished. Every cup of thirst-quenching water is a reminder that only Jesus can forever satisfy the spiritual thirst of every human being.

The Way to the Heart of True Productivity

Identify Your Limits

It's one thing to accept that we have limits and that this is a good thing; it's another thing to identify exactly what they are. Although we all need to eat, sleep, drink water, and exercise (among other things), we do not all need to do so to the same extent or in the same way.

For example, I am an extremely early riser. I really enjoy starting my day early. My energy levels are at their highest at five o'clock in the morning. By midday I start to notice that my creativity begins to wane, and by six o'clock in the evening my brain goes into a kind of automatic mode. I find any kind of creative work after that time to be extremely difficult. After years of trying to work at different times of the day, I have realized that the best way to harness my energy is to do my creative work in the morning and manual labor (such as cleaning the house or preparing food) in the afternoon.

In addition to physical limits, it's also useful to identify our psychological limits. Because I do not find it difficult to speak in public, many are surprised to discover that I am quite introverted. This means that I use up a lot of energy when I spend an extended time in situations where I have to interact with a large number of people. It's important that you and I take these kinds of personality traits into account in the context of a social or church gathering. Of course, my introversion is no reason to stop worshiping with other Christians or to isolate myself from those around me, but it does pay to prepare for the days when I have to meet with a lot of people.

Other people may have limits regarding diet, exercise, mental or physical illnesses, medications, learning difficulties, and more. It's important that we are aware of every boundary and do not see them as something we have to escape from in order to be productive but as a place where we can be productive. Some limits are universal (we all need sleep) and others are more particular (some need to avoid certain foods); some limits are transient (struggling to solve a problem after a large meal) and others are permanent (only having twenty-four hours in a day). Be that as it may, in the midst of any kind of limit we can use what we have to honor God and serve our neighbor.

Plan according to Your Limits

It's crucial that, when planning our day, we take into account not only the clock but also our physical and mental limits. As

I mentioned earlier, I tend to experience my energy levels at their highest during the early morning hours. For this reason I try to go to sleep relatively early and schedule most of my thinking and meetings for the morning and midafternoon. If I don't, it's easy for the evening hours to become a time of procrastination and unproductivity. Being an early riser, the best use I can make of the early hours of the night is to sleep. This way I am full of energy in the morning and can use this time to work on my mentally demanding tasks.

It's important that after you identify what time of the day you experience optimal levels of energy, you try to organize your activities to make the most of these levels. Of course, not all of us have the same flexibility of schedule, and in some chaotic seasons of life there is no choice but to sleep where you can and when you can. That's all fine and good. But, as far as possible, try to identify what time of the day you experience optimal levels of energy and use this to complete the most important tasks of the day. Even a small change can make a big difference (e.g., avoid using your cell phone until you have done your most important task in the morning). Leave the more routine tasks (such as cleaning or answering emails) for times when your energy is waning.

Another example might be of a mom during her first months of parenting. In general, this season of life is extremely routine and often leads to isolation. In the case of an extroverted woman, all this can be particularly difficult to cope with. To fulfill the natural need for social interaction, this mother could plan her week so that every two or three days she can go out to meet with other mothers of young children. She might even make it one of her priorities to ask for help from time to time so that someone can watch her children while she goes out to socialize with other adults in a more relaxed way. When organizing your to-do list and calendar, use your boundaries to establish how many responsibilities you can take on and the time frames within which you can fulfill them. Don't fool yourself into thinking you can function at 100 percent all day long. You're a human being, not a robot (and even robots need to have their batteries charged from time to time).

Learn to Say No

To plan with your limits in mind, you will have to get used to using the word "no." Obviously, you will have to say no when other people ask you for things that are beyond what you can handle. But the most important thing is to learn to say no to yourself.

When the temptation comes to log on to my social media in the morning instead of doing my most important task of the day, I have to say, "No, Ana." When I am reading a very intriguing novel that could absolutely consume my entire workday I have to say, "No, Ana." When I want to rationalize my decision to skip my thirty minutes of exercise and watch TV instead, I have to say, "No, Ana." When I want to spend the whole night writing instead of getting some rest, I must say, "No, Ana."

You are the person you spend the most time with, so you are the person who can most hinder your own path to true productivity. Learn to identify when you're being tempted to step beyond your boundaries, stop, and say no.

Now, saying no to yourself is easier than saying no to others. You don't have to worry about perceiving yourself as rude (just don't forget to preach the gospel to and not be too rough on yourself when you think about your struggles!). However, when we say no to others, things are very different. Depending on the culture you live in, saying no in a straightforward manner can be more or less complicated. Here are some ideas that may help you:

1. *Take your time.* Many yeses that we later regret come from rushing to give an answer. Do not feel obligated to respond to every request immediately. Say something like "Thank you so much for considering me for this! Give me a few days to think about it and I'll let you know if I can do it." Give yourself time to pray, consider your current responsibilities, and discuss your options with two or three people you trust. Give an answer only when you're convinced of what you're going to say.

2. *Be polite but firm.* Some people are afraid to say no because they feel that only "important" and "busy" people can afford to decline the requests of others. No. Your time, energy, skills, and focus are just as important as those of others. You must use them wisely. You can politely and firmly decline without feeling guilty.

3. *Make your no very clear.* Depending on who you are talking to, you might take three paragraphs or one sentence to deliver your no. Whatever you do, make sure that when you say no, you say it very clearly. Don't ignore the message, avoid the question by changing the subject, or, worst of all, say yes and then not do what you promised to do. Be grateful for the opportunity and state your answer clearly. Let no one be in any doubt that you will not do what you were asked to do.

4. Avoid giving explanations. You don't need to convince anyone that your no is justified. That is between you and God (and, if you're married, your spouse). Many people will try to convince you that you can adjust your schedule to accommodate their request (and others will want to make you feel guilty!); don't get too caught up in this. Say "No, thank you" as many times as necessary.

5. Offer alternatives. A good way to soften the impact of your no is to steer the person in another direction in order to find someone else. This doesn't mean illegitimately passing the buck but rather finding someone who is better suited for the task. Another alternative is to tell the person to ask you again later, when your schedule is less busy.

6. Remember that a no can be temporary. There are many things we dream of doing that we can't do at any given time; saying no can feel like turning down a once-in-a-lifetime opportunity. It doesn't have to be that way. There are seasons of life when we will have to say no more often, but let's keep in mind that that "no" may actually mean "not yet." Saying no is important not only for big requests but also for everyday requests. Remember, every activity, no matter how small, consumes our resources. Let's make sure we don't ignore our limits by taking on more than we can handle. Only then will we be able to do the right things the right way.

Recognizing my limits reminds me that God is God and I am only one of his creatures. He is the only one who can hold the universe in his hand; he is the only one who knows every detail and fulfills his purpose without fail all the time, orchestrating all the events of the universe according to his will. Recognizing my limits moves me off center stage and takes a huge weight off my shoulders. I am not the one who is going to put all things in order—I am a small thread in the great tapestry of redemptive history. I have the privilege of being here and making changes in the world, of transforming the lives of those around me through ordinary acts of love and service.

The to-do list never ends. There will always be emails to answer, dishes to wash, articles to write, customers to call, and students to teach. The needs of this world are unending. Although it's painful to admit, we cannot supply them all. We only play a small part in all that God is doing to restore the universe. Recognizing the reality of our limits does not prevent us from accomplishing the good works that God has prepared for us to do (Eph. 2:10), but trying to play every possible role *does* stop us from doing what we have to do and doing it well. Every believer has a part to play in this mission, and we are all equally valuable.

No human being was designed to carry the weight of the world on their shoulders. Jesus alone bore all the sins of his people. He was crushed by our wickedness so that we, even given our human limitations, could walk in freedom.

For Reflection

1. Which of your human limits are you most prone to ignore? Why?

2. How would your productivity change if you embraced that boundary?

Action Points

Identify the boundary you are most likely to ignore and write down three practical ideas that can help you respect it. Here are some examples:

- Go to bed at the same time every night
- Make a healthy meal plan for the week
- Say no without giving explanations

6

Decisions

Good news: you don't have to do it all.

EVERY TIME I ENTER A BOOKSTORE, I have mixed feelings. I am filled with sadness and joy at the same time. You see, in any one bookstore there is only a tiny percentage of all the books that have ever been published in history. Still, the shelves are packed with novels, scientific essays, biographies, and more. Being in the midst of all those books reminds me of how little I will be able to read in my lifetime. Thus, visiting a bookstore fills me with joy because I get excited at the thought of all that I can learn from the infinite number of pages that surround me, but it also tends to fill me with sadness because no matter how hard I try, I will never be able to read all the books I want to read.

Maybe you know that feeling. There are many things you want to do, many goals you want to achieve, and many places you want to visit, but time is limited—not to mention money and energy.

Even our skills (though we can develop them) seem to be lacking what we need in order to achieve everything we dream of. In our youth we don't want to believe it, but with time we accept it: we can't do everything.

This might discourage us, but it doesn't have to be that way. Realizing that we can't do it all doesn't have to turn us into bitter people with shattered dreams. We have limits because we need to be continually reminded that we are not at the center of history. We will not be able to perform all roles, but we can rejoice in doing the part God has called us to do the best we can. We can't do everything, but that's okay: we don't have to do everything. Being a thread in a tapestry can be disappointing if we only see ourselves. However, our attitude changes when we appreciate the beauty of the threads around us and rejoice in the way we all weave together to form something much greater than ourselves. We are privileged to be part of something infinitely more glorious than anything we could ever achieve on our own.

A productive life is a life that seeks to honor God with all that it has. Understanding this can fill us with joy: all of us can be productive because we can all seek to honor the Lord. But understanding this might also fill us with paralyzing sadness. We see our limited resources—time, talents, energy, money, and more—and we don't even know where to start. We understand that we have time to do everything we should be doing, but how can we know what that is? Should I enter university or set out as a missionary to a distant country? Does God want me to marry this person or that person? Is it a good idea to look for a new job or should I stay where I am?

In our eagerness to find the right path, Christians turn to the Bible. The problem is that we tend to do it the wrong way. When we want to make an important decision, many of us use Scripture as a kind of crystal ball: we want one of its verses to tell us exactly what to do, when to do it, and how to do it. We have learned that, in one way or another, God will use the words of the Bible (accompanied by a "strong impression in your heart" or an "open door") to tell us whether we should be a youth leader or a worship leader, have two children or seven children, or study communications or health sciences.

In the book *Just Do Something*, Kevin DeYoung explains that there are three ways we can talk about God's will. The first is called his decreed will, which is basically anything that happens in the world. The Bible says over and over again that everything that happens, happens only because God allows it. He has absolute control over the universe, including the most insignificant details of our lives, such as the individual hairs that fall from our heads (Matt. 10:30). This does not mean that God is the author of sin and evil but that he temporarily permits them in order to fulfill his eternal redemptive purposes. After all, if God were to eliminate all sin and evil from the earth in an instant, we would be eliminated as well.

On the other hand, we have God's will of desire, which is what he has revealed in the Scriptures. These are the specific commands about how we are to live. DeYoung explains that God's decrees tell us "how things are, [and] the will of desire is how things ought to be."[1]

---

1   Kevin DeYoung, *Just Do Something: A Liberating Approach to Finding God's Will* (Chicago: Moody, 2009), 21.

The third way we can speak of God's will is his will of direction, reflected in the question, What exactly does God want me to do right now? The will of direction is usually what we are most concerned about, although, ironically, God never promises to direct us in this way.

I won't deny that sometimes I wish everything was simpler. It would be very practical if God would speak to us by phone or send us an email with a detailed list of everything we need to do each day. Although obeying would probably be just as difficult (after all, our rebellious hearts would still be the same), at least we could know exactly what God expects of us, even in the everyday details of life. We would not have to deal with uncertainty and fear of being wrong. But God has not decided to speak to us in this way.

Of course, Christians have all that they need in Scripture to live in godliness, but in the Bible, we do not find a direct answer as to whether we should start a construction business or enroll in seminary. Sometimes we want to use Bible verses to justify our decisions, but let's be honest, "Be strong and courageous" (Josh. 1:6) can be used either to stay in your current job or to look for a new one. Using verses out of context to make a decision will always depend on how you feel: are you more afraid of your boss or the challenge of entering a new workplace? Experience and the Bible tell us that feelings are not always reliable when making decisions (Jer. 17:9).

The Bible was written for us but not primarily to us. It's a mistake to ignore the original recipients of the text as if the Scriptures had reached our bedside table without first crossing many millennia and civilizations. To say that God has called you to be a preacher because you read, "I appointed you a prophet to the nations" in Jeremiah 1:5 might be the equivalent of reading Jonah 1:2, "Arise, go to Nineveh, that great city," and wanting to set sail for Mosul.[2] Of course, although these kinds of commands in the Bible were not given to us in a particular way, we can still distill principles from them to help us make godly decisions in our own context. Although God has not called me to preach to Nineveh like Jonah, he has called me to make disciples of all nations (Matt. 28:19–20), proclaiming the gospel even to people I might consider my enemies. But this is very different from saying that God wants you to be a millionaire king because you happened to read about Solomon's majestic reign in 2 Chronicles 1 when you were praying for direction for your life.

Overall, Scripture isn't only for me but for every believer in the history of the church, from the first century to the end of the centuries and from the Middle East to the islands of Oceania. In its pages we find the story of a creator God forming a people of forgiven and restored sinners for his glory and for eternity. The Bible isn't a treasure map wherein God has hidden the specific plans for my life, waiting for me to solve a bunch of puzzles in order to finally obey him. The commands and promises of Scripture are not fortune cookies to be consulted at random every time we must make an important decision. Rather, the Bible is the word of God that reveals the person of God to the people of God. To understand its message we need to read it completely and in context; we err when we use the Bible as we please to support the decision we want to make, and we also err when we live paralyzed in fear just because we have not found the right verse to act on.

---

2   The present-day city in Iraq where the ruins of Nineveh are located.

So, what do we do? If God does not offer us details about what to study in college, what job to take, what ministry to serve in, who to marry, or how many children to have, how do I know what I should be doing?

The Way to the Heart of True Productivity

God does have a plan for our lives because we are created with purpose. He wants to glorify himself and extend his kingdom through each of his children. We have the privilege of using all our resources to show the world who God is and what he has done for us, no matter who we are or how capable we feel. Every Christian is called to love God and his neighbor, making disciples wherever he goes. That is the essence of God's plan for our lives. But what about the details? We don't know them and we don't need to know them. God has given us the resources we need to live a life that pleases him, with the freedom to make holy choices. The Holy Spirit indwells each and every believer and guides them by means of the word, the church, and reason to identify the things they should be doing.

Fill Yourself with the Word of God

The Bible is the place where God reveals to us who he is and what he has done. In it, we learn what holiness looks like. On the one hand, we find direct instructions that apply to all believers in all places throughout history, such as "pray without ceasing" (1 Thess. 5:17), "do not commit adultery" (Luke 18:20) and do not neglect "to meet together" (Heb. 10:25). On the other hand, we learn that there are many other matters in life that require wisdom since "all things are lawful, but not all things are helpful" (1 Cor. 10:23).

Although the Bible will not give us specific answers for the decisions we must make in daily life, it does transform our minds to become people who test what is God's "good, pleasing, and perfect will" (Rom. 12:2). God's children know his voice and follow it. And although God has not promised to give us all the details of the journey (Deut. 29:29), he does give us the direction: "If anyone would come after me, let him deny himself and take up his cross and follow me" (Matt. 16:24).

Scripture isn't a book we open every time we are afraid of making a wrong decision. Scripture is our source of light for each day, through which God conforms us to his image more and more to make decisions that honor him, in the big things and the small. We need not attach so much importance to subjective impressions of our hearts ("I feel like God is leading me to do this") or to supposedly open doors ("I was given the opportunity to do that"); after all, our emotions can be deceptive and God-dishonoring opportunities can arise (like Jonah's boat!). Our job as believers is to obey God's will as clearly revealed in Scripture and to seek wisdom for everything else.

Pray for Wisdom

The Lord knows your heart and knows if your desire is to honor him with your decisions. He knows your limitations and knows that sometimes you're confused by the choices you're facing. God isn't waiting for you to take a wrong step that will ruin the perfect plan he has prepared for you. Rather, he promises to fulfill his purpose in you and bring you to the end no matter what.

In sum, God's will is our sanctification—to be made more and more into "the image of his Son" (Rom. 8:29; see 1 Thess. 4:3). He isn't sitting on a cloud waiting for us to make good decisions for this will to be fulfilled. On the contrary, the apostle Paul exhorted the Thessalonians concerning this reality when he wrote, "May the God of peace himself sanctify you completely, and may your whole spirit and soul and body be kept blameless at the coming of our Lord Jesus Christ. He who calls you is faithful; he will surely do it" (1 Thess. 5:23–24). The Lord is always working through our decisions to make us into the people he wants us to be and to extend his kingdom in our midst.

Thus, when we pray for wisdom to make decisions that honor God, we are asking for something that we know he delights to "give generously" and "without reproach" (James 1:5). Just as we must continually feed on the word, so must we continually pray that the Lord will shape us into wise and courageous people who make decisions according to the word of God.

Ask for Help

Human beings were not made to be alone. We all have blind spots and sometimes it's difficult for us to honestly see our true motivations or abilities, which is why we should remember that "in an abundance of counselors there is safety" (Prov. 11:14). One of the best things we can do to walk in wisdom is to surround ourselves with a group of close friends and family members who love the Lord and can be completely transparent with us. These people can listen to our desires, help us pray for opportunities, and offer their perspective on the situations we face.

Yet, although it's imperative that we heed the advice of wise and godly men and women when making important decisions, we must be careful. Many of us are so afraid of making a mistake that we become completely dependent on what others say and are unable to act for ourselves. But no human being is infallible. Thus, it's a terrible mistake to turn the voice of your parent, pastor, boss, or leader into the voice of God. Listen to their advice, but don't forget that it's very important that you know the Scriptures for yourself. If you're a Christian, remember that the Holy Spirit dwells in you and gives you direction and strength to discern and walk in wisdom.

Make Decisions and Walk Faithfully

Once you have meditated on Scripture, prayed, and listened to the counsel of others, the only thing left is to make a decision. There are times when making a choice will require a few weeks; in most cases we can make decisions relatively quickly. But I must warn you that sometimes we clothe our fear in piety. We are terrified to make mistakes and months go by without taking any steps because "we keep praying about it." Or we get desperate and start looking for signs everywhere. This isn't necessary. I repeat, God has not hidden secret codes in the Bible or anywhere else. You are free to choose (provided, of course, that your decisions do not contradict the direct commands of Scripture) and to faithfully walk in the direction you have decided to take.

There will be times when you realize that you have not made the wisest decision. Maybe you said yes to teaching a Sunday school class but you didn't consider all the time you would need to prepare and now you're neglecting your job or your family. Or maybe you've started a degree that you're not really enjoying. That's okay. These things happen. It might be time to make another decision: should you continue in this major or withdraw in a responsible manner? We can honor God even when we have to take a step back.

In book five of his *Confessions*, Augustine of Hippo recounts the moment when he left Carthage to settle in Rome. Augustine was not yet a believer and the last thing on his mind as he embarked on this journey was to honor the Lord; in his words, he was seeking an "unreal happiness."[3] Yet, after his conversion, Augustine reflected on how God used even his perversity to bring him to the place where he needed to be: the country where he would become a Christian. In a prayer of praise, the theologian acknowledges, "You alone, O God, knew the cause of my going thence and going there."[4]

We do not know where the decisions we make will lead us, but we do know that God is using them for his glory and our good. As we face the future, we can rest in the truth that the Lord's plans are much higher than ours and that he will fulfill them regardless of our limitations or failures. God has given us everything we need to walk in godliness. We have nothing to fear. Let us walk seeking wisdom and seeking to make the best use of our resources. God will glorify himself with every step we take.

For Reflection

1. With what you have learned so far, do you think we can fulfill our mission (loving God, loving others, and making disciples) through decisions we make that do not directly relate to church ministry? How?

3 Augustine of Hippo, *Confessions*, bk. 5, chap. 8
4 Augustine, *Confessions*, bk. 5, chap. 8

2. Recall some of the most important decisions you have made in your life. How has God been glorified through them?

3. Meditate on some of the things you *should* be doing according to the Bible (e.g., staying in the word and in prayer, worshipping with other Christians, making the gospel known). How can you adjust your schedule or integrate these into your daily life to give them the priority they deserve?

4. Think of a decision you're afraid to make. What is stopping you from taking action?

Action Points

Draw four columns on a sheet of paper. In the first column, place the things you're doing. Write down all the projects that come to your mind, whether they relate to work, ministry, or your personal life. In the next column write down the things you would like to be doing. Write down all the activities that you're interested in doing but have not taken the time to include in your daily life.

Over the next few weeks, reflect on these two columns and start making decisions. Are there things you can eliminate or postpone? Take the steps you need to take to finalize or delegate the commitments you feel you should no longer be working on. As you complete these, cross them off your list. If there are any projects that you can postpone for later, put them in the third column: things to do later. Finally, transfer (little by little) all the projects that you're convinced you should be doing right now to the fourth column.

7

Focus

If you don't keep your eyes on the goal,
you will end up getting lost.

THE "THORNS AND THISTLES" of the twenty-first century are not usually thistles and thorns (Gen. 3:18). The difficulty of our work seems very different from that faced by the majority of people who have dedicated their energies to tilling fields and raising livestock. Social media managers deal with trolls, and physicians with difficult diagnoses. As a writer, my thorns and thistles are the limitations of my own reasoning; my eternal struggle is with the jumbled ideas in my head. If my son could talk, he would say that mom's job is to look at a shiny rectangle with a frown on her face.

That's why I want to escape. Concentrating isn't easy. Even when I remove all distractions—notifications off, phone locked, sound-proof headphones on—my mind wants superficial entertainment.

As I write, I want to stop writing. My eyes want to stray from the target because running to the finish line is painful. Of course, falling or getting lost is painful too, but future Ana can take care of that. For now, I just want to distract myself.

It's good to know that we have time to do what we should be doing. It's great to understand that we can't do everything and we don't have to. However, there is no point in identifying all the things that we do have the privilege of doing if in the end we do nothing. And what do we need in order to do right things the right way? Focus.

To focus is to keep our attention on something in a deliberate fashion in order to fulfill an objective. It's the opposite of what we usually do when we instinctively respond to the stimuli around us. Instead of honing in on one thing, we jump from one thing to the other without giving it much thought and in the end achieve absolutely nothing.

We like to think that we can put our attention in several places at the same time without affecting the activities we are doing. But our brain does not have that capacity. We can only do two things at the same time when one of the things we are doing is so habitual that we do not need to think about it to do it (for example, listening to a book while walking or doing the dishes). Beyond that, "multitasking" is just a myth. What we are doing is switching activities rapidly, fragmenting our attention in all directions instead of truly placing our eyes on the task in front of us.

This reality humbles us. To use our focus correctly we must admit that we cannot do everything at the same time. Yet, this reminds me, once again, that I don't need to do everything at the same time. Since "for everything there is a season" (Eccl. 3:1), we are free to put all our focus on what it's time to do now. If we are working, we can focus on working. If we are resting, we focus on resting. As I write this book, I must fight the temptation to distract myself by checking my phone every time I run into some difficulty in expressing my ideas. As I play with my toddler, I must fight the temptation to get caught up in the anxious thought that tomorrow I have to write at least three thousand words if I want to finish my projects on time. Once I know what I should be doing, my responsibility is to focus on that task and perform it to the best of my ability, glorifying God in my work and in my rest.

For some unknown reason, humans cannot walk in a straight line without visual cues. In a series of experiments conducted by psychologist Jan Souman, he observed that participants walked in circles instead of in a straight line in places where the landscape looked the same all the time, such as on a cloudy day in the woods or in the desert. When participants' eyes were blindfolded, their trajectory became even more erratic, and they ended up walking in much smaller circles.[1] No matter how hard they tried to walk in a straight line, the participants ended up completely lost when their eyes were not fixed on something.

The same thing happens to us, both in the sublime and the everyday. It's for good a reason that the Bible tells us to "run with endurance the race that is set before us [by] looking to Jesus" (Heb. 12:1–2). When we are not making sure that our sights are set on the goal, we end up getting sidetracked, worrying more about temporal things than eternal ones. No matter how organized my schedule is, my inner self will not be able to focus on what it should until I rest

---

1   Laura Mcguinness, "We Can't Help Walking In Circles," NewScientist, August 21, 2009, https://www.newscientist.com/.

in the Lord. With our eyes fixed on him we can do the tasks before us knowing that we are making progress toward the goal. Moreover, in day-to-day life, much of our stress arises not because we don't know what we should be doing but because when we do know, we are tempted to set our sights on other things.

R. C. Sproul wrote that "right thinking and right doing can be distinguished from each other, but they can never be separated."[2] To use our attention correctly we must think correctly about our attention. The first thing we must learn is that our attention is valuable. Along with your time, your attention is one of the most precious resources you have. Today we live in the attention economy; companies like Meta and Google are among the most lucrative in the world despite the fact that their services are free because they sell the attention that we give them in abundance to advertisers on their platforms.

The Way to the Heart of True Productivity

Attention is like a muscle: we must exercise it. Astronauts on the International Space Station must average two hours of daily exercise to compensate for the lack of resistance of a zero-gravity environment. Otherwise, they would lose their muscle and bone mass. In our hyperconnected age, you and I are in the same situation. We live life in emails, text messages, and fifteen-second videos. We have lost much of our ability to focus on something for an extended period of time.

The analogy holds when we think of the effort required to exercise our attention. It's difficult and painful. Our desire is to

2 R. C. Sproul, *The Consequences of Ideas: Understanding the Concepts that Shape Our World* (Wheaton, IL: Crossway, 2018), 31.

give up quickly because the results are not immediate. But we need to persevere. There is a war for our attention. It's crucial to spend time teaching our mind to resist in the depths rather than fleeing to distraction. How? The following ideas are a good place to start.

Spend as Little Time as Possible on the Superficial

Every moment we spend on the superficial affects us. Cal Newport, author of *Deep Work*, writes, "Spend enough time in a state of frenetic shallowness and you permanently reduce your capacity to perform deep work."[3] This should awaken us to the importance of every small decision we make regarding our attention.

Every experience we live through shapes our brain in a tiny but real way. If we live in the superficial, surrounded by impulses that demand our attention at every moment, our mind will lose the ability to focus on deep things. It's like when a child spends hours and hours in front of the television: he loses the ability to find fun in the world around him and finally just wants to be entertained. Avoid becoming a brain that only wants to feed on the sugar of the superficial.

This, of course, does not mean that you can never relax and have fun. On the contrary, it means that you should seek to relax and have fun with things that are worthwhile. And when it's time to rest, focus on enjoying that rest.

Make Room for Depth

In a world like ours, where infinite distraction is literally at our fingertips, it takes intentionality to spend time in the depths. This

---

3 Cal Newport, *Deep Work: Rules for Focused Success in a Distracted World* (New York: Grand Central, 2016), 17.

means eliminating all optional distractions during certain times of the day so that you can focus on the important things ahead of you that require more of your attention. Try the following exercise:

1. Choose a valuable activity you want to give your full attention to. It can be reading, writing, playing with your child, having a conversation with a loved one, playing an instrument, or preparing an elaborate meal.

2. Determine a period of time during which you will devote your full attention to this activity. It can be as short as five minutes or as long as an hour depending on your current attention span, the nature of the activity, and the time you have available in your schedule. Don't reach for the stars. Five focused minutes are better than forty scattered minutes. Gradually, you will be able to increase your focus time.

3. Block out all distractions that compete for your attention. Don't depend on your good intentions. Rip out things that could become temptations (Matt. 5:29). In his book *Atomic Habits*, James Clear writes, "The people with the best self-control are typically the ones who need to use it the least."[4]

4. Focus on what is in front of you. If your mind starts to wander, return to your goal. If some difficulty arises that makes you want to flee to distraction, pause. Breathe. Remember that it's only five or ten minutes. Stop if you have to, but whatever you do, do not give in to distraction.

4   James Clear, *Atomic Habits An Easy and Proven Way to Build Good Habits and Break Bad Ones* (New York: Penguin, 2018), 93.

Every decision you make in favor of focus will make you stronger.

5. Rest and repeat. Paying attention takes a lot of energy, so don't be surprised if your mind is tired after concentrating on something difficult for a long time, especially if you're not used to doing it regularly. Cal Newport, an expert in what he calls "deep work," says that a person like him can only do this kind of extreme focus for about four hours a day. Repeat this exercise as many times as you can. You will see that you will improve with practice.

Keep Your Spiritual Eyes on the Goal

Learning to concentrate on ordinary things is of little use if we do not learn to concentrate on sublime things, running toward the goal with our eyes fixed on Jesus. And the easiest way to set our eyes on the eternal every day is by developing spiritual disciplines. We will talk more about habit formation, including habits of grace, in the next chapter. For now, it's worth mentioning that Bible reading and prayer are two basic practices that lead us to take our eyes off ourselves and our problems and place them on the Lord.

Human beings are forgetful. We take three steps and our gaze begins to wander. We need to continually recalibrate our heart so that we do not get lost as we run the race of faith.

In the twelfth letter of *The Screwtape Letters*, written by C. S. Lewis, the demon Screwtape writes to his apprentice Wormwood about a strategy to gradually cool the heart of the Christian they want to destroy. Screwtape assures him that the more gently they divert the believer from looking to God, the better. Over time, it will become easier and easier for the "patient" to be distracted from looking for the "enemy." The demon writes,

> [Then] you will find that anything, or even nothing, is sufficient to attract his wandering attention. You no longer need a good book, which he really likes, to keep him from his prayers or his work or his sleep; a column of advertisements in yesterday's paper will do. You can make him waste his time not only in conversation he enjoys with people whom he likes, but also in conversations with those he cares nothing about, on subjects that bore him. You can make him do nothing at all for long periods. . . . All the healthy and outgoing activities which we want him to avoid can be inhibited and nothing given in return, so that at last he may say, as one of my own patients said on his arrival down here, I now see that I spent most my life doing in doing neither what I ought nor what I liked.[5]

It's not difficult to imagine the strategies that Screwtape would recommend to his nephew in the twenty-first century. Let it not be said of us that we spend little time on what we ought and like to do. Let us treasure our focus and put it on what is worthwhile. Let us rest in the fact that, although our troubled hearts often crave the immediate satisfaction of distraction, God still calls us to himself and offers us grace to move forward when we fail. Let us seek to live a deep life, in work and rest. Let us invest our attention in what will last for eternity.

5 C. S. Lewis, *The Screwtape Letters: With Screwtape Proposes a Toast* (New York: HarperCollins, 2001), 60.

For Reflection

1. Have you noticed how your day changes when you try to focus on heavenly things before doing anything else? Describe this in a short paragraph.

2. How do you react when faced with a difficulty at work? Do you escape to some form of distraction?

3. How do you plan to respond after reading this chapter? What measures can you implement to make it easier?

Action Points

Establish a regular daily time to exercise your attention. Choose an activity and focus: set an alarm and avoid running to distraction until it goes off. Remember, the period for the alarm to go off does not have to be very long. The key is to be consistent.

8

Habits

Every step in the right direction counts.

MY BODY REFUSED to work the morning after my first day at the gym. But I dragged myself to the mirror and looked. I turned to one side and looked again. I squinted my eyes, looking for some evidence that the day before I had spent forty-five minutes on a bicycle going nowhere, but found none. I thought about giving up. What's the point of all this effort if there's not going to be any change?

This is, of course, a fictitious scenario. I fully understand that developing my physical condition through exercise and a healthy diet only produces visible changes gradually. Weeks, if not months, must pass before we are able to notice any change on the outside. Inner changes come a little faster, but still, at the beginning everything seems to get worse: my muscles are so sore that I can barely move, and I run out of breath just by spending ten minutes on the elliptical trainer. However, I am gradually discovering that I have more energy than before. My stress levels have begun to decrease and I even perceive the world more clearly. Little by little I am realizing that developing the habit of exercise pays off.

While it's easy to recognize the absurdity of expecting immediate results when it comes to exercise, it's harder for us to realize that the same is true of personal productivity. We decide to get organized or spend less time on our phones, and we get down to work. We download apps and spend all afternoon watching videos that teach us how to prioritize our to-do list. We try to follow the strategies but then realize that it's not as simple as we had imagined. After a couple of days, we give up; we go back to the same old routines, convinced that we were simply not born to be productive people. But being productive isn't about finding the perfect tool to keep your schedule under control. Rather, being productive is being transformed day by day into a person who uses what they have for the glory of God and the good of others.

How are we transformed? The answer may disappoint you. To a large extent, it happens through our daily habits. The things we do on a regular basis are what make us productive or unproductive people. Although we dream of immediate and extravagant changes, becoming productive is a process that takes place gradually over time through our daily activities. God uses ordinary means to do extraordinary things in us.

For better and for worse, every human being is a creature of habit. This is for the better because habits free our brains from the daily burden of making thousands of decisions by doing so automatically. This is also for the worse because we often fail to realize how our daily practices mold us into people we don't really want to be.

We all have good habits (brushing our teeth before going to bed), neutral habits (the way we tie our shoes), and bad habits (looking at our phones immediately after waking up). The problem is that we don't give them much thought. Why is this a problem? Because bad habits—the patterns of behavior that have a negative effect on our lives—are the easiest to form and the most difficult to eradicate. They usually have an immediate reward and their negative effects may go unnoticed or be attributed to something else. They make us believe that this is just how life is and blind us to the reality that we can make a change for the better. Together, these characteristics form a lethal combination that causes bad habits to invade practically all areas of our lives without us noticing.

If you wake up and the first thing you do is check social media, you'll feel great for a while. It's very likely that afterward you will feel guilty because you have wasted two hours on the phone, and you will try to do something productive. But everything you consumed during your time on the phone will still be buzzing around in your head, and you will feel the strong impulse to go and check it for any news you do not want to miss. All this makes you fall into a spiral of procrastination that will last for the rest of the day. Before going to sleep you will make a promise to yourself that you will not do it again. No more checking the phone right after waking up. Yet, you make the mistake of leaving your phone in the same old place with the same old apps ready to provide you with the same old entertainment. You're convinced that you can resist temptation. But the morning comes and everything you have to do during the day comes to your mind. You want to escape the worry for just a moment, so you pick up the phone and the cycle starts all over again. A small, seemingly harmless decision made on a consistent basis has turned you into a person who spends the first few moments of the day offering your valuable time and attention in exchange for a little superficial entertainment—a person you don't want to be and don't have to be but that your habits make you.

In addition to the use of our phones in the early hours of the morning, there are hundreds of small daily decisions we make that alter the course of our lives. It sounds a bit dramatic, but it's true. James Clear uses the example of the flight path of an airplane. If a pilot leaves Los Angeles airport with the intention of arriving in New York but changes his direction only 3.5 degrees south, the plane will end up in Washington, DC, some three hundred and sixty-two miles from his destination. Clear writes, "A small shift in direction [of the aircraft] can lead to a very meaningful change in destination."[1]

When we talk about productivity, we tend to set idealistic goals without realizing that our daily practices take us in the opposite direction. We say, for example, that we want to keep our affairs in order. We want to be able to know what things we should do every day. That is the goal. But how are we going to achieve it? If every time a new responsibility comes along at work you have a habit of simply saying, "Okay, I'll take care of it," and then forget what you were asked to do, you're walking in the opposite direction of your goal. The solution is to visualize your goal and

1 James Clear, *Atomic Habits: An Easy and Proven Way to Build Good Habits and Break Bad Ones* (New York: Penguin, 2018), 17.

chart a path of habits that will lead you toward it. If you want to get organized, you could start by designating a space for each item on your desk and develop the habit of returning each tool to its place when you're done using it. At first it will be difficult, but little by little it will become as natural as it used to be to leave those things anywhere else. It's these kinds of small habits that, over time, will lead us to become the productive people we want to be. As James Clear writes, "Every action you take is a vote for the type of person you wish to become."[2]

We underestimate the power of perseverance, both in the good as well as the bad. Small but steady steps are much more effective in getting us to our goal than an occasional big leap. An important aspect of productive living is learning to identify small changes that, over time, can transform the way we use the resources we have to love God and others. The productive person seeks to develop simple practices that will lead them in the right direction.

Suppose Carol wishes to cultivate her depth. She has found that she can only concentrate for a few minutes each time she tries to sit down to read. What habits could she develop to grow in this area? Here are a few examples:

- Carol could turn off her phone at seven o'clock every night in order to spend a few hours each day without the many distractions it provides.
- Carol could set an alarm for ten minutes, during which time she must devote herself solely to reading, resisting

2   Clear, *Atomic Habits*, 38.

the urge to distract herself with something else. Gradually, her attention span will be strengthened and she will be able to increase the time she spends reading.

- Carol could block off two hours in her daily planner to process her to-dos from start to finish, seeking to complete each task one at a time instead of trying to do several things at once.

These simple practices are small steps (or habits) in the right direction (to not get distracted when reading). You may have noticed that two of the habits Carol could implement have nothing to do with reading, but by strengthening her attention span, they will inevitably affect the way she reads.

In his book, *Keep in Step With the Spirit*, theologian J. I. Packer explains a bit about the importance of habits in Christian sanctification, the process through which we are progressively set apart from sin and become more like Jesus. Packer writes that "habit forming is the Spirit's ordinary way of leading us on in holiness."[3] Holy habits make us holy people and sinful habits make us sinful people. This does not mean that sanctification is a human work but that God has decided to use our own efforts as part of the process. Packer states,

> Holy habits, though formed . . . by self-discipline and effort, are not natural products. The discipline and effort must be blessed by the Holy Spirit, or they would achieve nothing. . . . Holiness by habit forming is not self-sanctification by self-effort, but is

3   J. I. Packer, *Keep in Step with the Spirit: Finding Fullness in Our Walk with God* (Grand Rapids, MI: Baker, 2005), 90.

simply a matter of understanding the Spirit's method and then keeping in step with him.[4]

The race of faith is a marathon that lasts a lifetime. God isn't going to teleport us to the finish line. Thus, our calling is to put one foot in front of the other, again and again, until we complete the journey. And behind every step is God himself, sustaining and directing us.

The most important holy habits are our spiritual disciplines. In fact, these crucial practices of the Christian life are also known as "habits of grace."[5] Donald Whitney defines spiritual disciplines as "those practices found in Scripture that promote spiritual growth among believers in the gospel of Jesus Christ."[6] Whitney lists ten disciplines, including Bible reading, prayer, evangelism, and silence. Each of these disciplines, carried out regularly and in the power of the Spirit, is used by God to transform our character for his glory and the good of others.

This directly affects our productivity. If productivity is a matter of character—a character of faith, purpose, diligence, and depth, like that of our Lord—then productivity is tied to our sanctification. The more God conforms us to his image, the more productive we are. Our character is formed on a daily basis through the many decisions we make every day.

---

4 Packer, *Keep in Step with the Spirit*, 91.

5 David Mathis, *Habits of Grace: Enjoying Jesus through the Spiritual Disciplines* (Wheaton, IL: Crossway, 2016), 15.

6 Donald S. Whitney, *Spiritual Disciplines for the Christian Life* (Colorado Springs: NavPress, 2014), 4.

Habits make productive living second nature. Christians want honoring God to be a daily lifestyle, and that is precisely what habits are all about. Goals can give us a direction to aim for, but good habits (i.e., small, everyday productive practices) are what will get us there.

The Way to the Heart of True Productivity

Create a Favorable Environment

Good habits are not formed by wishing them into existence. If our natural tendency were to cultivate them, the whole world would live a productive life all the time. But the reality is that if you want to develop your character through the development of productive habits, you will have to make changes, starting with the physical spaces around you.

To develop good habits, you don't have to rely on your will-power alone. In fact, the less you need to use it, the better. It's true that the world we live in is full of distractions and junk food, but the same does not have to be said of our own home or workplace.

Let's make our physical environment a place that supports productivity, small oases that promote honoring the Lord. Create the best environment you can to live the life you want to live. If you don't want your first activity after waking up to be looking at your phone, turn it off and put it in a drawer; stop putting it on your nightstand (yes, it's time to buy an alarm clock). If you want to read more, surround yourself with books and unplug the TV to make it harder to turn it on automatically. If you want to learn to play the guitar, put it in the center of the room next to everything you need to practice. If your goal is to have devotions every morning, leave your Bible and prayer journal on your desk the night before. If your goal is to stop being distracted for hours watching videos on the Internet, install an application to block websites. If you want to eat healthy, stop buying junk food and fill your refrigerator with fruits and vegetables.

Don't set yourself up for failure. Don't expect to overcome the temptation of distractions by having them in front of you at every turn. Organize your desk, your room, your cupboard, and any space you can to encourage the development of good habits.

Choose Key Habits

There are particular habits that can radically change your life for the better. These are simple practices that affect other areas of your life almost without you realizing it.

For example, it's a very good idea to get into the habit of washing your plate immediately after eating. However, it's unlikely that this practice will result in drastic changes beyond a well-ordered kitchen. On the other hand, a habit like Bible reading and meditation first thing every morning can completely change the tone of your day. Other key habits are things that make you physically stronger, such as exercising or eating more vegetables. Developing these types of practices will give your body more energy to better fulfill your responsibilities. Here are more ideas for key habits:

- Reading
- Praying
- Planning your day
- Eating less sugar

- Getting enough sleep
- Going to bed and getting up at the same time every day
- Drinking enough water
- Tidying up the house before going to bed

Focus on One Habit at a Time

When you read a book like this, it's normal to feel excited and want to transform your life overnight. Avoid falling into the trap. Immediate radical changes tend to not last long. It's better to go slowly but surely.

But do not despair. Choose one habit and focus on it until it becomes a natural part of your routine. By definition, a habit requires little or no reflection to perform—it's a *habitual* activity. You must wait until that point, until it's no longer difficult to perform the habit, before you start developing a new one.

Some say it can take a certain amount of time to develop a habit. The reality is that there is no specific number of days written in stone; how long it takes you to develop the habit depends on the habit and how regularly you practice it. With practice, you will improve in developing these habits and even be able to work on several at the same time.

But it's best to start with just one thing and resist the desire to change your whole life overnight. Start with a small change. Just as we don't want to start by making a lot of changes at once, we also don't want to start by making changes that are too big and unsustainable over the long haul. When we want to create a new habit we usually set out in high spirits but after a few days realize that overcoming our habits isn't easy, so we end up abandoning the practice we wanted to develop.

I like to say that to cultivate a good habit you have to be mediocre. For example, someone who has never read a book might set a goal of reading two minutes a day. It sounds like a ridiculous goal, and it's quite likely that anyone sitting down to read can read for more than two minutes. But that isn't the point. The key to developing a habit is to be consistent; we are much more likely to persevere with a new practice if sticking to it is very easy. Reading two minutes every day and remaining consistent is better than reading for an hour but only when you feel inspired.

Do the Best You Can

When we hear about habit development, many of us immediately become defensive. "Yeah, sure, I'd love to get eight hours of sleep, but my kids won't let me." "It would be wonderful to develop a habit of reading, but I don't even have money for books." "Of course I want to eat healthy, but I have to eat what's available."

Developing good habits is easier for some than for others. There is no doubt about that. Some people have more flexibility to change their routines because of their economic or family situation. Yet, despite the obstacles, we can all make small changes that will help us to be a little better off than we were yesterday. We do not need to set aside an hour each day to develop a new habit. We simply have to do the things we already do but in a different way. Identify one of your bad habits and try to transform it into a good one. For example, if you're in the habit of eating a bag of potato chips on your office break, replace it with an apple. Or if you relax with thirty minutes of social media when the kids go to sleep, why not try using your phone for only fifteen minutes and then using the rest of the time to read a good book? There will always be obstacles to our productivity; our calling is simply to do the best we can with what we have.

Last, don't forget to ask for help. If you're a mother of young children, you could make an arrangement with a friend to take care of them while you study the Bible. If you find it difficult to exercise consistently on your own, enlist a friend to go for a walk with. After all, "two are better than one" (Eccl. 4:9).

Be Patient and Do Not Forget the Gospel

Changing our behavior takes time and effort. Without realizing it, we have spent our entire lives developing practices that impede our productivity. It's important not to be too hard on yourself. Persevere. Remember, God is the one most interested in transforming us. If my productivity isn't for selfish reasons, I can be assured that God will bless my efforts to develop habits that will bring me closer to the goal: to love him and to love others, making disciples wherever I go.

When we fail—and we will fail—we must remember that our value and identity do not lie in how well we develop healthy habits. We can work hard to create practices that help us better use our resources for the glory of God and the good of others, but we can also rest in the fact that the ultimate transformation of our heart is the work of the God of the universe. For him, nothing is impossible.

For Reflection

1. Think about what you did yesterday. On a piece of paper, write down all of these activities (e.g., waking up, drinking coffee,

checking your phone, reading for a while, brushing your teeth, and so on) and identify the good, bad, and neutral habits.

2. What kind of person would you like to be in ten or twenty years? Are your daily practices leading you in that direction?

3. What changes could you make in your home or office to encourage better habits?

Action Points

Choose a good habit you want to cultivate. If spiritual disciplines—particularly Bible reading and prayer—are not a regular practice for you, start there. Then, follow these steps:

1. Decide when, where, and how you will carry out this new discipline.
2. Prepare the right environment to develop this new discipline.
3. Determine an accountability method for supporting this new discipline.

Here is an example using the habit of Bible reading:

1. I will read the Bible every morning at seven o'clock in the dining room, using a yearly reading plan.
2. I will print out the reading plan and keep it in my Bible. Before going to bed, I will place my Bible and prayer journal in the dining room. I will make sure the coffee pot is ready before going to bed.

3. Each time I complete my daily reading, I will check it off in my habit-tracking application. On Friday afternoons I will write to a friend who also wants to cultivate spiritual disciplines and we will talk about the week's challenges and victories.

9

Tools

Your brain was created to create, not to store.

"I CAN'T FORGET TO CALL HIM."

"Ah yes, sure, see you Friday!"

"I'll deliver this to you tomorrow without fail, don't worry."

The end of the day is coming and there is a lot on our minds—small fragments of scattered information. No wonder we feel so overwhelmed.

Systems and tools are usually the first things we think of when we talk about productivity. But we have left these systems to the end of the book for a good reason. Downloading and learning to use different tools for personal productivity does not make you a productive person. Rather, productive people use tools effectively and build systems that help them be who they already are, enabling them to honor God and love others by making the most of all their resources.

If the biblical goal of personal productivity isn't simply to have tasks organized but to love God and love others, our productivity tools are not just our calendars, to-do lists, electronic devices, or other tools we use at work. All objects around us can be tools for productivity. My books help me learn new things in order to serve others by writing resources like this one. Good dinnerware can be useful in providing a nutritious meal to neighbors who are struggling financially. On the other hand, just as a hammer can be used to hurt someone or to build a house, so can many objects around us be used to destroy rather than to love. I can use my books to gain a lot of knowledge in order to humiliate someone; I can use my dinnerware to feed only those I consider worthy enough to share my table.

The temptation to use the good gifts that God has given us (including the ability to use tools) for unproductivity is something that has haunted humanity for a long time. Yet, this does not only refer to lazy people lying in bed all day but also anyone who misuses productivity. For example, we can build unproductively, as seen in the story of the beginnings of humanity in Genesis: Human beings organized themselves very well and worked hard to erect a building that would take them to heaven and make them famous. In doing so, the builders of the Tower of Babel corrupted their minds and their hands. They had been made in the image of God, with the ability to create marvelous tools, but they used those tools to rebel against the God who had given them his image.

It's our responsibility to use the gifts and tools that God gives us for his glory. Again, we can build or destroy. The tools Noah used to build the ark may have been very similar to those used by the builders of the Tower of Babel.

The most obvious equivalent for us is probably our phones. Cell phones are incredible tools. A few decades ago, it was unthinkable to be able to do everything we do with these small, luminous rect-angles. We can see the faces of loved ones who live oceans away. We can find the best route to reach the hidden gems of our city. We can learn practically anything we want to for free and from the comfort of our home. We can find out what is happening right now almost anywhere in the world, hearing the voices of those who suffer injustice and pain.

Without a doubt, our cell phones are incredible tools. But they can also be black holes that swallow our productivity. They are deceptive tools because they are not passively there waiting for us to use them as we see fit. In one way or another, they drive our behavior. They are designed to attract our attention and to be used at a certain time and in a certain way. The developers of our favorite apps work hard to keep us on the screen as long as possible, even if we have notifications turned off. Cell phones and social networks have become a very integral part of our society, to the point that it seems we would not belong to the community without them. Using our phones well is a challenge. We need wisdom to determine how we can use the objects around us for productivity (true work and true rest) and not to satisfy our selfishness, to reflect the image of God and bring order in the midst of disorder.

In fact, using your tools unproductively may not look very different—at least on the surface—from using your tools produc-tively. A bed is an excellent place to rest. Someone who is living the biblical passage that says God "gives to his beloved sleep" (Ps. 127:2) does not outwardly seem very different from someone who needs to be rebuked with the question, "How long will you lie there, O sluggard?" (Prov. 6:9). But God looks at the heart. The productive person uses the tools at their disposal to contribute to the building of God's kingdom by loving and serving those around them.

Overall, human beings were created to create. Our brains were designed to take the things that are on earth and tap the potential of the world for the glory of God and the good of others. We do this at home, at work, at school, at church, and in our neighborhoods. We do it by designing buildings or marketing plans, writing laws or novels, changing diapers or the plumbing in a building. And tools allow us to extend our brain's capabilities and do the things we are called to do more effectively.

In the following pages we will be concentrating on the two tools that are traditionally most associated with personal productivity: the daily planner and the task list. These are tools most people would benefit from but rarely think about how to use. For example, during his professional training, a photographer learns the right way to use his camera as a tool to capture unique moments and convey inspiring stories. However, it's highly unlikely that he is taught how to use tools that will help him make good use of his time and attention to continue capturing moments and conveying stories. It's a shame that tools that can be so beneficial are so often overlooked.

With each passing year our lives seem to become more complicated. There are always errands to run, meetings to attend, messages to send, emails to respond to, meals to prepare, reports to write, and orders to pick up. If we try to keep it all in our heads, it won't be long before we feel completely overwhelmed. The calendar and the to-do list serve to store the things we have to do and specify the time when we will do them.

Why do we need these tools? They help us store crucial information about our productivity and get into work mode more efficiently. The to-do list tells us what we will do, and the daily planner tells us when we will do it.

You'll know you're using these tools the right way when you don't have to wake up every day trying to figure out what you should be doing—you simply look at your daily planner and to-do list and are ready to work. Getting to that point takes practice and patience, but when you reach it, you will find that the effort has been worthwhile. Your brain will be free from the stress of remembering each of your pending tasks, and you will be able to use all your energy to do the things you need to do in the best way you can.

The Way to the Heart of True Productivity

Use What Works for You

For a long time, I wanted to force myself to use paper planners. I saw pictures of fancy notebooks, colorful highlighters, or decorative stickers, and I wanted my personal organization tools to look like that. But after years of empty planners and frustration, I decided to admit it: what works best for me are digital tools.

Maybe your preference is the opposite of mine. You've tried downloading a lot of applications and none of them help you keep your tasks and meetings in order. You prefer to carry a physical notebook and write down what you have to do by hand. Maybe it even helps you remember things better. That is excellent. Use what works for you.

If you don't know where to start, follow your instincts. Most of us can identify whether we prefer pencil and paper or electronic devices. Whether in a physical or digital format, get a daily planner and decide where you will write down your tasks. For now, you don't have to worry too much about which planner or task management system is the best. Just choose a tool that you want to use frequently.

Practice Using Your Tools

Before we start organizing priorities or canceling unnecessary meetings, we need to get in the habit of regularly using our productivity tools.

First, make sure that you're entering information into your task manager and daily planner, otherwise they will be of no use to you. This habit, like all habits, is acquired with practice. If you use digital tools, place them on the main screen of your cell phone. If you prefer paper, try to carry your planner with you everywhere you go. When a task or meeting comes up, write it down immediately. It doesn't matter if you end up turning down the appointment or delegating the task. It's better to delete a useless piece of information than to forget an important piece of information. Another option is to carry a piece of paper in your pocket, write down any pending issues and appointments that arise, and then transfer them to your daily planner or phone at the end of the day.

In order to get into the habit of regularly reviewing your daily planner and to-do list, set a reminder on your cell phone for each morning and evening. Take five minutes to review your notes, eliminate what is no longer useful, and familiarize yourself with what you will be doing over the next few days.

Distinguish between Tasks and Projects

In his book *Getting Things Done*, productivity expert David Allen teaches the importance of distinguishing between tasks and projects. A task is any simple activity that can be completed in one sitting: a phone call, answering an email, doing the dishes, and so on. A project is any activity that requires two or more tasks to complete: preparing a presentation, reorganizing a closet, writing an article, and so on.[1]

One of the main reasons for our frustration in trying to complete things we need to do is that we fail to distinguish between projects and tasks. Your to-do list is a list of tasks, not projects. For example, the "write an article" project includes tasks such as writing an outline, gathering research sources, reading and taking notes on the sources, writing the first draft, writing the second draft, editing, and so on.

It's okay to put projects temporarily on your to-do list so you don't forget them. However, at least once a week you should identify all the projects you have during a given month and divide them into their component tasks. Each step you need to take to complete the project should be placed on your task list with a specific due date.

Let's practice with this example by placing the project due date on our daily planner (preferably before the actual due date) and working backward by assigning each task in the days leading up to the due date in order to complete the project on time (see figure 2).

---

1 David Allen, *Getting Things Done: The Art of Stress-Free Productivity* (New York: Penguin, 2001).

SUN	MON	TUES	WED	THURS	FRI	SAT
					1	2
3	4 Outline and collect sources	5	6 Read and take notes	7 Read and take notes	8	9 Write first draft
10	11 Write second draft	12	13 Edit article	14 Submit article	15	16

Figure 2. Task due dates

Organize Your Priorities

Once you have become accustomed to using your productivity tools on a regular basis and have made sure that your to-do list is really a list of tasks (not projects), you can begin to better organize each item.

A key step is to identify whether the items on your list are urgent or important. An urgent task is one that must be done immediately or in the very near future. An important task is one that will contribute to the advancement of your projects and goals.

Each morning, select one important task from your list as the priority for your day. This task will be the one that will receive your time and attention first; the others will wait until the priority is completed. Once you are done with this task, you can continue with other items on your list. If you need help deciding what to do with each of the tasks on your list, use the famous Eisenhower Matrix (see figure 3).

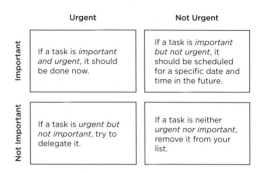

Figure 3. The Eisenhower matrix

Plan Your Time

Some productivity writers argue that we should avoid adding tasks to our calendars. They say that your daily planner is exclusively for matters that have to be carried out at a specific time and place, such as a doctor's appointment. I do not agree. Depending on how much control you have over your schedule, the daily planner can be a great place to put your tasks at a specific time of day.

To plan your schedule, you must be able to recognize the amount of time that a task will occupy. This is also the best way to avoid long to-do lists. By planning our time, we recognize that it is limited and that we are only able to accomplish a certain number of tasks each day. Here is a list of steps you can follow to put this into practice:

1. Review the tasks you have for the next day and enter the estimated time it will take you to complete each one.
2. Add fifteen to thirty minutes to your estimate (we tend to be overly optimistic when we think about the time it will take to complete our unfinished business).

3. Place specific blocks of time for each task in your daily planner.

If you prefer to be flexible with the order in which you perform your tasks, don't add the blocks of time to your daily planner. Simply use the planner to see how much you can do in a day.

On the other hand, if the many interruptions in your work do not allow you to establish a fixed schedule for each task—if you're a mother of young children, for example—you can use a strategy called block scheduling.[2] This consists of dividing your day into different thematic blocks of time that can last three to four hours (see table 1). For the duration of a given block of time, you will be limited to doing as many activities as you can within the category assigned to it.

Table 1. Example of a block schedule

Morning	Errands	Afternoon	Evening	Night	Sleep
6:00-9:00	9:00-12:00	12:00-3:30	3:30-7:30	7:30-10:30	10:30-6:00
Devotions Breakfast Get ready for school 30 mins of cleaning and organization	Go to the supermarket Run errands Go to the library Go for a walk with kids Visit friends	Lunch Kids sleep or play in their room Study Work on personal projects	Spend time with family Dinner Wash dishes Put kids to bed 30 mins of cleaning and organization	Watch TV Read Organize for tomorrow Exercise Bathe Work on personal projects	Sleep

2   Jordan Page, "The 'Block Schedule' System," August 30, 2018, YouTube video, https://www.youtube.com/.

Planning in this way makes us aware that every activity we perform is carried out over time. Just as we budget wisely to manage the money in our bank account, we must also face the reality of how much time we have available and where we are spending it. See an example of a schedule and corresponding task list in figure 4.

	SCHEDULE	NOTES	TASK LIST
5 a.m.	Get up, make coffee, and get dressed Breakfast		5 mins. Reply to email (Frank) 10 mins. Reply to email (Martin) 60 mins. Cook and eat 5 mins. Reply to email (Joan) 30 mins. Tidy Up 60 mins. Meeting with Robert
6 a.m.	Tidy up as much as possible		
7 a.m.	Write report		Read Article Brainstorm event ideas Call John Fold clothes
8 a.m.	Rest Meeting with Robert	15 minutes; read or go for a walk Don't forget to write action points	
9 a.m.	Rest	15 minutes; read or go for a walk	
10 a.m.	Small tasks Meeting with Margaret		

Figure 4. Schedule and task list

Use Additional Productivity Tools

Once you're well acquainted with daily planners and task lists, you can start using other tools to leverage your resources. Here are some that I use:

- Habit log: to make sure I am consistent with simple, habitual practices that lead me in the right direction, such as reading, drinking enough water, exercising, and so on (I use *Streaks*)
- Email manager: to communicate with my work team and receive important information (I use *Spark*)
- Cell phone blocking: to spend as little time as possible on social networks and other distractions (I use *Forest*)
- Note organizer: to store all kinds of important information, such as PDF documents, addresses, and my weekly plan in a safe place (I use *Notion*)

If you have never used a to-do list or a calendar to organize your activities, familiarizing yourself with these productivity tools on a regular basis may take some time. There will be days when you will completely forget to check your notebook. You may find that the tool you thought would work for you didn't work in the end. That's all fine; it's part of the process. Just don't give up.

Try to use the same tools for at least a couple of weeks just to be sure that you're giving them a chance. If after that period of time you still feel that they are not helping, identify why. Do the features of digital task managers seem too complicated, but you don't want to use paper? Perhaps you can start by jotting down your to-do items on your phone's default notes app. Do you forget your planner in a corner of the house? Maybe you can carry a piece of paper in your pocket to jot things down that come up during the day and then, in the evening, take some time to organize everything in your notebook. Identify what you need to get your mind organized and adjust what you need to adjust in order to get those functions from a tool.

Whatever you do, don't give up. Be flexible but consistent. Use the tools at your disposal to free up your mind from having to remember unfinished business so you can concentrate on doing the things you have been called to do to the best of your ability. You don't need to live in the stress of day-to-day life, figuring things out as they come up. Sit down for a while and start planning. I'm sure your brain will thank you.

For Reflection

1. Look around you and select three objects that are close to you. How could you use these objectives for the glory of God and the good of others? How could you use them unproductively?

2. What has your experience been like in trying to organize your pending projects and meetings? After reading this chapter, how do you think you could improve in this area?

Action Points

If you don't use productivity tools, try keeping a planner and a to-do list for at least two weeks, either in physical or digital format. Enter your meetings and pending tasks as they arise, and set reminders on your phone to check your planner and to-do list every morning and evening.

If you already use productivity tools, make sure that all items in your task list are actually tasks and not projects. Take some time each night to evaluate your pending tasks for the next day and determine their importance and urgency. Before going to bed, decide what your priority task for tomorrow will be.

PART 3

———————

PRACTICES

10

Align Your Life

Desire that your life count for something great!
Long for your life to have eternal significance. Want
this! Don't coast through life without a passion.

JOHN PIPER

MANY OF US ARE WAITING for something extraordinary to happen in our lives so that they will become something worth talking about. The reality is that God makes glorious lives by means of a lot of everyday moments. Our existence is already valuable. We don't have to do anything to earn the Lord's favor; Christ has clothed us with his righteousness and in him we have "every spiritual blessing" (Eph. 1:3). Productivity simply helps us to participate in the privilege of using all that we have in the great story of God the creator, savior, and servant. He is restoring all things for his glory and our good; it's our joy to be a thread in this beautiful tapestry.

Some Christians think that planning isn't worth it because God is sovereign and, at the end of the day, he can do whatever he wants with our lives. It's true that God is sovereign and that he can do whatever he wants with us. His plans are much better than ours—there is no doubt about that. However, this does not mean that we should not plan. Rather, Scripture calls us to do it the right way: by fixing our eyes on the Lord and surrendering our desires to him (Prov. 15:22; 16:3, 9). When we do it according to the Bible, planning can be an act of faith. When planning, Christians seek to honor the Lord with the resources he has given them while keeping their hands open, recognizing that what he has planned is far better than anything they could imagine.

In previous chapters we learned that God does not offer a treasure map with the specific plan for our life hidden somewhere inside. But even if we do not have detailed instructions, we must get to work, like the servants in the parable of the talents. We don't have to try to guess what God wants for us beyond what is laid out in the Bible or wait for some angelic voice to tell us what to do. We can plan and act. We can look at what God has given us, decide wisely where we want to go, and find a path that takes us in that direction.

Where Do You Want to Go?

When we think about our productivity, we tend to focus on the day-to-day. It's good to take one step at a time, but to make a good plan, we also need to look at the big picture. I like to do it at three levels:

1. Horizon (two to three years)
2. Goals (six to eighteen months)
3. Projects (up to six months)

The horizon is the direction you want your life to go in the coming years. It can be a work or home horizon. If you choose something work related, it doesn't mean you're going to ignore your family for the next three years. It simply means that the area you're focusing on growing in right now is your job.

Goals are medium-term objectives that take you toward the horizon. At this stage, select about five goals that will make you grow in your horizon. These goals will be worked toward one by one.

Projects are smaller activities that contribute to the fulfillment of your goals. You can have several projects of different sizes going on at the same time. Below is a list of four hypothetical people and their horizons, goals, and projects that serve as examples of how to do this.

Sophia

1. Horizon: to create a spiritual support organization for children
2. Goals: design creative content with social impact; create a collaborative team; begin a course on theological training
3. Projects: participate in a drawing workshop; read a book about early childhood education; read a book about organizational leadership; create content proposals; design a creative project plan

James

1. Horizon: to stabilize our family's finances
2. Goals: complete a personal finance course; pay off credit card debt; save for an emergency fund

3. Projects: enroll in a personal finance course; keep a spending log; create a family budget; write a will

Josh

1. Horizon: to go as a missionary to Guatemala
2. Goals: complete a course in Spanish; get a work visa; save enough to live in Guatemala for six months
3. Projects: read about Guatemalan culture; create a yearly budget; design a fundraising plan; identify possible local churches; identify possible living accommodations

Rebecca

1. Horizon: to improve parenting skills and fix broken things in the house
2. Goals: organize house; establish routines for each child; polish their table manners
3. Projects: clear out the closets; clear out the kitchen; design a meal plan; read a book on parenting; prepare educational activities

Overall, the objective of writing down your horizon, goals, and projects is to specify the direction you want to walk in and the steps that will take you there. This doesn't mean that the only projects you will take on will be those that contribute to your goals and horizon. After all, we have jobs to attend to and families to love. Rather, this exercise will simply help you get a better idea of where to focus your efforts and make it easier to say no to things that take you away from your goals.

If you find it difficult to think about your horizon, ask yourself the following questions: Where am I right now? What are the responsibilities God has given me at home, at work, and at church? How can I grow to better fulfill these responsibilities? What would I like to be doing three years from now with the talents God has given me?

You can also ask your spouse, pastors, or other people you trust questions like, What do you think I am good at? How do you think I could grow in the next three years? Do you think it makes sense for me to try to take on this project or major in this degree?

Once you have defined your horizon, brainstorm your goals. What goals can you accomplish in six to eighteen months that will help you move in the right direction? Write down all the things that come to mind, at least twenty items. Then select the five that you consider most relevant. Be realistic about what you can achieve in the coming months. You can save the rest of the goals you wrote down for later. For now, have just those five on hand so you can concentrate on reaching them one by one.

Finally, think of some projects that you need to carry out in order to accomplish your goals. For example, if your goal is to pay off debt, you can include projects like making a budget, reading a personal finance book, or starting a savings account so you don't have to use your credit card in an emergency. These projects will go alongside the projects you probably already have at home and at work, which we discussed in the previous chapter. The challenge for you will be to give your personal projects the importance they deserve and seek to make steady progress on them.

Don't be afraid to dream. Don't be afraid to want things for the glory of God and the good of others. Set your eyes on the Lord and offer him all that you have. Delight in God and let him guide you through his word in order to use your resources in a way that fills your heart and serves others.

> Trust in the Lord, and do good;
>> dwell in the land and befriend faithfulness.
> Delight yourself in the Lord,
>> and he will give you the desires of your heart. (Ps. 37:3–4)

For Reflection

1. What direction would you like to head in over the next three years?

2. Are you doing anything right now to move in that direction? If your answer is yes, what are you doing? If not, why are you not doing those things?

3. What things are you doing on a daily basis that don't contribute to your goals?

Action Points

Determine your horizon, your goals, and your projects.

11

Plan Your Week

*I resolve never to waste a moment of time, but
to use it in the most profitable way possible.*

JONATHAN EDWARDS

MOTIVATION COMES and goes unpredictably—except on January 1. There is something special about the new year that makes us look forward to what is to come and motivates us to make all the changes we know we should make. The rest of the year, motivation comes and goes without warning, so I don't like to rely on it to take action. But when I feel motivated, I'm going to take advantage of it. It's not a bad thing to use that clean slate feeling to start acting differently.

Employing a weekly plan is a way to have that clean slate feeling without having to wait for the new year. It's a space where, on a regular basis and no matter how terrible your week has been, you can pause and start again. It's a way to evaluate your time, boundaries, decisions, focus, habits, and tools in order to redirect you to the center of productivity. Investing time to put together a simple strategy may be all you need to feel ready to take productive action through the week. As James Clear writes, "Many people think they lack motivation when what they really lack is clarity."[1]

Your weekly plan is a simple and personal checklist you go through on a regular basis before the start of the workweek. Once you finalize your plan, you will know exactly what to do and when to do it. At the same time, you will organize your activities so that they can be adjusted in case of emergencies or unexpected urgent tasks.

No two weekly plans will be alike, but they should all have three essential components:

1. Neutralize: In the first part of your weekly plan, you will review all the information and tasks you received in the previous week and organize them.
2. Evaluate: You will then look at what things you need to focus on over the next week.
3. Plan: Finally, you will identify what you will do over the next week and determine when you will carry out your activities in a concrete but flexible way.

Design Your Own Weekly Plan

Below is an illustration of my weekly plan (see table 2). Once you observe what I do, create your own weekly plan, taking

---

1   James Clear, *Atomic Habits: An Easy and Proven Way to Build Good Habits and Break Bad Ones* (New York: Penguin, 2018), 71.

into consideration your routine and work tools. The entire list may seem overwhelming, but examining one part at a time will help you realize that designing your own weekly plan is easier than it sounds.

Table 2. Weekly plan checklist example

1. Neutralize	2. Evaluate	3. Plan
(a) Pray	(a) Review goals	(a) Organize tasks for
(b) Update prayer	(b) Review monthly	the week
requests	calendar	(b) Define priorities for
(c) Empty inboxes	(c) Review projects	the week
i. Email		(c) Make a meal plan
ii. Messaging app		(d) Time blocking
iii. Paper trays		(optional)
(d) Tidy up		
i. Desk		
ii. Digital devices		
iii. Clean devices		

It's your turn. Select a one-hour slot at the end of your work week; be specific about the day, time, and place. This will be your time to plan. Protect this space and ask for help from your family if necessary. Put it in your daily planner and set up reminders; do whatever you have to do so that you don't forget. Remember that this planning time is an investment that will help you better serve your family, co-workers, and members of your church. Prepare a text document wherein you can create and store your own weekly plan. If pen and paper are your thing, you can use a planner. You will go through the same checklist every week so it's a good idea to create it in a place where you can easily duplicate it. Now, let's discuss in more depth the three essential components mentioned above using the example of my personal weekly plan.

Neutralize

PRAY

I begin each weekly plan by remembering the gospel. Maybe the previous week was a disaster. I must free myself from everything that did not depend on me and repent for everything that was my fault (maybe I was lazy or sought to be in control without considering others). I seek to be honest with my sin and rest in the fact that God is faithful and just to forgive me in Jesus. I can move forward. On the other hand, I may have had a very good week. What had to be done got done and I was able to enjoy some rest with my family.

In both cases, I thank the Lord and look to him before I dive into to-do lists, emails, and daily planners. After all, "the plans of the heart belong to man, but the answer of the tongue is from the LORD" and if you "commit your work to the LORD, [then] your plans will be established" (Prov. 16:1, 3). Through prayer, I align my desires with the Lord's desires. I can lay out my plans and hopes, surrendering them to God and recognizing that, at the end of the day, his plans are much better than mine.

UPDATE PRAYER REQUESTS

In my prayer notebook I keep sticky notes where I write the requests I pray for during my devotions. During my weekly planning session, I text some of the people I have been praying for to ask them how they are and to find out what God has been doing in their lives. I then discard the prayer notes that need to be discarded and update the prayer notes that need to be updated.

EMPTY INBOXES

The next step in my weekly planning session is to review all the places where I store information and tasks to make sure nothing gets lost. I open my email and messaging applications first. If appointments were made, I make sure to put them on my calendar. If there is important information, such as addresses or PDFs, I put it in my note organizer (right now I use *Notion*). If I find to-dos in any emails, I put them in my to-do list application. If during the week I entered information into my *Notion* or *Todoist* inbox (my task management app) but didn't organize it into the right folder or project, now is the time I do so.

TIDY UP

Once my information is where it needs to be, it's time to get everything else in order. If my desk is full of books and stationery that I used during the week, I throw old sticky notes in the trash and put the books back on their shelves. I do the same in the digital world. I make sure my computer desktop is clear, deleting the files that need to be deleted and placing the rest in their proper folders. When everything is in order, I physically clean my laptop and other electronic devices.

All of this is only overwhelming the first time you do it. If you organize your devices on a weekly basis, you will find that it only takes a few minutes to put everything in its place. The clarity you get when everything is in order makes it worth investing in that first session when nothing has a designated spot yet.

———

It's your turn. Make a list of all the places where you receive information: email, physical mail, messaging apps, productivity apps, and so on. Then identify the workplaces where you spend the most time during the week. It can be a table in your office, a corner in the kitchen or dining room, or even a shelf in your bedroom where you store your books and stationery. Try to do your weekly planning in the same spot so you can leave everything in order at the end of each week. If you have prayer lists or anything else you need to review regularly (e.g., a list of books to read, places to visit, or recipes to try), include them in the neutralize section of your weekly planning.

Evaluate

REVIEW GOALS

I prefer habits to goals, but I will not deny that the latter help us make progress in the right direction. For this reason, I try to have important goals that I know I must be working on continuously. I try not to have too many each year (five is more than enough) and I only work on one at a time. In this section of the weekly planning session, I review my list of goals for the year and remind myself of what I am focusing on right now. This helps me avoid attempting to do everything at once (the rest of the goals are there and will eventually get the attention they deserve) and ensure I am making progress toward the main goal.

REVIEW MONTHY PLANNER

When I neutralize my inboxes during the week, I will have placed all my meetings and deadlines on my calendar. Now it's time to review what's coming up in the month. What things should I keep in mind over the coming weeks? And what things should I do this week in order to be ready for upcoming meetings and deadlines? Here I simply take a sheet of paper and start writing down the things I need to keep in mind for the next seven days, forgetting about everything else.

REVIEW PROJECTS

In chapter 9 we made a distinction between tasks and projects. A task is any simple activity that can be completed at one time. A project is any activity that requires more than two tasks to be completed. During my weekly planning session, I make sure to review the projects I am working on in order to make sure I am performing tasks that will keep each of them on track. A list of projects at the bottom of your weekly plan may be sufficient. In this step of my weekly planning session, I take the same sheet of paper from the previous point and write down the tasks to be carried out next week for each project.

———

It's your turn. In your weekly planning document, make a section for yearly or quarterly goals. Aim for three to five goals.

They can be things like finishing a Spanish class, reorganizing the closets in the house, or getting a raise at work. Make sure they are realistic goals for the time frame you're giving yourself.

To stay on top of your meetings and deadlines, use your daily planner regularly. It doesn't matter if you feel you have too few commitments. It's important to have a visual guide to your time so that you can make better use of it. If a paper planner doesn't work for you, try a digital one, and if you don't like digital planners, try paper planners. Make sure that all your appointments and deadlines for the next month are clearly visible.

Then, make a list of your ongoing projects right now and a list of possible future projects. The condition for your projects to be considered "in progress" is that you perform at least one task per week that leads to the project's completion. If you feel you have too much on your hands, move some of your projects to the future projects list. Remember that it's better to do a few things right than many things wrong. Focus diligently on just a few things and, in the long run, you will see that you can do more and better. After you have evaluated your projects, commitments, and deadlines, write down everything you need to focus on during the week.

Plan

ORGANIZE TASKS FOR THE WEEK

At this point, I can sort out everything I wrote on my sheet of paper in the evaluation section. I put all the tasks for the week on different days of the week in my task management application. If I notice that there are too many things, I move the least urgent to next week. The ability to determine how much you can do each day is acquired only with practice; in the beginning we will always try to do more than we have time and energy to do. Here, it's key to remember to not feel bad about how much we can get done in a week. We must embrace our limits—we are humans, not robots—and do the best we can with what we have.

DEFINE PRIORITIES FOR THE WEEK

Once I have all my tasks for the week ready, I choose three of them (at the most) that must be completed within the next seven days. I write them on a sticky note that I then put in a visible place. These tasks will receive my time and attention before the others.

Once I have accomplished these tasks, I can concentrate on the others. They are usually difficult but important tasks I need to accomplish in order to make progress on my projects and goals. The temptation will always be to fill my day with easy tasks that don't help me move forward with my goals, so having the week's priorities in a visible place helps me keep my eyes on what's important.

MAKE A MEAL PLAN

Once I plan my activities for the week, it's time to plan what my family will eat. Doing this ahead of time saves me a lot of headaches during the week. I don't have to be thinking about what we are going to eat every day. I prepare what I can in advance (e.g., chop vegetables, freeze pancakes, and boil eggs) and do the rest in small blocks of time during the week.

TIME BLOCKING

I sometimes use a productivity technique called time blocking, explained in chapter 9. When I use this method, I take all the tasks of the day, or at least the most important ones, and assign them to a block of time on the daily planner. This helps me know exactly what I will do and when I will do it. I only block out time on my planner a day or two in advance so that I can respond to unforeseen events and move tasks to later in the week if things don't go as planned.

Another thing I block out on my daily planner is study time. Since I am no longer in college, I must intentionally make time for learning if I want to keep my axe sharp. I put some blocks of time in my calendar when I know I can sit down to watch a class or read educational materials. I generally use free virtual courses or scholarly books. Whatever it is, I select and organize the material in advance so that I can devote myself to study during the allotted time.

———

It's your turn. After you have gone through the evaluate section, get a sheet of paper to write down the tasks you should focus on during the week. Put them in order in your planner or task management tool. Try to determine how long each task will take you and distribute the tasks throughout the week, making sure to pay attention to your planner. If you have a lot of meetings or errands on a given day, don't expect to complete too many tasks that day. Remember that a day only has twenty-four hours and you don't need more.

Select at most three tasks to be completed during this week. If there are more than three urgent tasks, you should go back to part 2 and evaluate your projects because you probably have too many commitments. Establish when you will complete each of your priorities, and be sure to leave a little room for the unexpected.

If you're responsible for any ongoing tasks (such as cooking) make sure you plan what you're going to do during the week and prepare as much as you can in advance. Further, try to find space in your daily planner for an activity that strengthens your body or mind (e.g., reading, exercising, attending a workshop, or doing crafts). Don't overwhelm yourself by trying to do it every day. These don't have to take up long periods of time either. Twenty minutes is a very good place to start, and about two slots during the week can be very helpful. If necessary, ask for help in order to set that time apart.

Look at your planner and to-do list. You already have your action plan for the week!

Final Thoughts

Give It Time

Setting aside an hour a week just for planning may seem like a lot, but it's one of the best investments you can make. Productivity expert Brian Tracy says that for every minute you spend planning, you will save ten minutes in execution.[2] Although it's not an exact science, you can be sure that every moment you spend planning is a moment well spent. That said, it's important to be patient. Don't expect to design a weekly plan (see figure 5), implement it once, and have your life completely revolutionized from that point on.

2   Brian Tracy, "Tips to Structure Your Day," YouTube video, 0:17, https://www.youtube.com/.

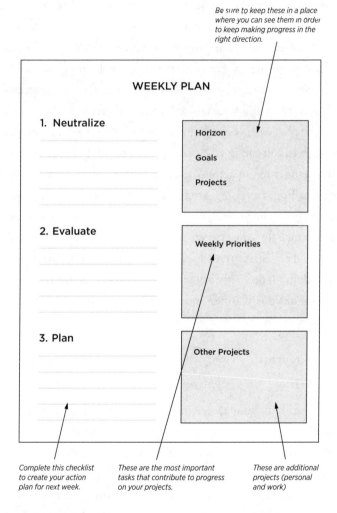

Be sure to keep these in a place where you can see them in order to keep making progress in the right direction.

WEEKLY PLAN

1. Neutralize

Horizon

Goals

Projects

2. Evaluate

Weekly Priorities

3. Plan

Other Projects

Complete this checklist to create your action plan for next week.

These are the most important tasks that contribute to progress on your projects.

These are additional projects (personal and work)

Figure 5. Weekly plan

As we learned earlier, productivity is a matter of character. Strategies such as the weekly planning session can help us, but they cannot transform us overnight. At first you will feel overwhelmed by all the unorganized documents and emails you have. You may struggle to get your daily planner in order and have no idea how to choose your priorities.

All of this improves with practice, but you have to persevere. Give time to your weekly planning session. Adjust the list of steps each week, adding or deleting steps as needed. If Wednesday comes and you haven't accomplished anything, take some time to make adjustments and move on. Don't give up!

Don't Get Frustrated by What You Can't Do

It's common for people who have very little control over their schedules (e.g., moms of young children) to feel that it's impossible to get organized. But this isn't entirely true. While it's true that motherhood forces us to be more flexible with our time, this does not mean that we cannot plan anything.

If your schedule is unpredictable, simply keeping your projects and their respective tasks in mind will help you know what to do when you have the time to do it. You may not know exactly when your schedule will allow time for reading, but if you plan your weekly reading ahead of time, you'll be ready to execute and follow through on it as soon as you get some free time. Planning, even a little and with plenty of room for flexibility, will always be better than not planning and spending your life dealing with emergencies.

Make Sure You Have Your Tools on Hand During the Week

It's common to get excited about a new planner but after a few days forget about it, only to find it in November crammed in a corner of the room. Don't let that happen to your weekly plan. For it to work, you must check it regularly.

Have your weekly plan, daily planner, and to-do list in one place that is easily accessible to you. Create a home for these tools on your device or desktop. If necessary, create reminders on your cell phone to review the plan every morning and evening.

If Your Plan Fails, Don't Fall Apart; Adjust and Move On

The weekly plan isn't set in stone. Although the ideal is that you stick to your plan as much as possible, things happen and you can't always do that. Sometimes it's our fault (like when you don't feel like working and end up watching two hours of videos on the Internet) and sometimes it's not (like when there's a family emergency). Repent of what you have to repent for, thank God for his grace, and move on. If it's necessary to make adjustments to your plan for the next few days, do so. If you need to take a few days of real rest (not laziness), go ahead! But whatever you do, don't stay crushed in defeat.

For Reflection

1. Before reading this chapter, had you ever tried to plan your activities in advance? What does a week that has been planned in your life look like in contrast to one that was not?

2. How do you respond when things don't go according to your plan? Do you get frustrated and give up or do you adapt?

Action Points

Design your own weekly plan. It can have any steps you want, but it should include the three sections introduced in the chapter: neutralize, evaluate, and plan. Test it for at least three months, adjusting as necessary.

12

Make the Most of Your Day

*How we spend our days is, of course,
how we spend our lives.*

ANNIE DILLARD

EACH DAY OF OUR LIVES is a step in the race of faith. The way
we spend our time will reflect where our heart is. Regardless of
how routine our activities are, we can perform them for the benefit of the community, the glory of God, and the good of others.

We have already talked about how to design the path to the
horizon where you want your life to be headed. We also looked
at how to organize your week to make sure you're walking in
the right direction. The only thing left to do is to act. This is
the simplest and at the same time the most difficult part. We
like to dream, but when we are in the reality of the day-to-day,
we forget that every action we take is a step either toward or
away from that dream.

Here are some of things to keep in mind to make the most of your day.

The Night Before

A productive day starts the night before. When my sisters and I were little, one of the most important things in our routine at home was taking out our uniforms for the next day. Every night I spent half an hour making sure my clothes were clean and ironed, shoes were shined, and backpack was ready with all my school supplies. Making sure every night that I have prepared everything I need for the next day is a habit I keep to this day. No matter how old you are, it definitely makes mornings less chaotic. It's worthwhile to think of simple things you need early the next day that you can get ready while you do a mundane task like brushing your teeth or putting away the dinner dishes. If you want to go for a walk, why don't you leave your tennis shoes by the door? If you want to read for a while, you could leave your book on the couch and the coffee pot on a timer. If you want to have a devotional time, have your Bible and prayer journal ready on the dining room table.

Another thing you can do before you go to sleep is review the next day's tasks and give some thought to how you're going to complete them. If you have prepared your weekly plan (see chapter 11), you know exactly what tasks you should be accomplishing each day. Depending on how strict you want to be with your schedule, you can either set aside a full-time block in your daily planner (see chapter 9) or use the first few hours of the morning to accomplish your most important task.

Finally, note which of your tasks require a lot of mental energy (reading, writing, solving calculations, designing, preparing reports, teaching) and which require little mental energy (answering emails, making calls, cleaning, organizing papers, attending meetings, running errands). This distinction is useful for when the time of day comes that you feel tired but must continue working.

In summary, before going to bed, prepare all the things you will need early in the morning and review your to-do list for the next day, identifying tasks that demand high or low energy, as well as your priorities.

At the Start of the Day

Many of us live responding to the urgent because we do not stop to reflect on what is important. Your alarm can be an excellent tool to fight the tendency to merely react to life events: one of the simplest but most significant changes you can make to your daily routine is to get up before you have to get up. Instead of rushing out every day to beat traffic or being woken up by a crying child, go to bed a little earlier and set your alarm earlier than usual. By doing this, you can create a time of tranquility before starting your daily activities. It does not have to be very long; fifteen minutes is enough to start with. Once you get used to getting up a little earlier, you can extend this time to forty-five minutes or an hour if you wish.

What can you do during this time? Well, it depends on how long you have. Some productivity experts recommend designing a routine for your morning that includes things like exercise, reading, journaling, hydration, and more. All of this can be very good but also very overwhelming to think about. You don't need a ten-step routine to start your day off on the right foot. I recommend that you start with a couple of very simple things: spiritual disciplines and daily tasks review.

The morning is no more spiritual than the afternoon. It's true that in the Scriptures we read about the beauty of seeking God early in the morning (Ps. 119:147; Mark 1:35), but we also see that Jesus himself prayed in the evening and at night (Matt. 14:23; Luke 6:12). In the Bible we don't find specific instructions that you should do your devotionals in the morning, but if you wish to do so, the quiet space you have prepared before your daily activities is the ideal time.

However, even if you prefer to use the afternoon for Bible study and prayer, don't miss the opportunity to dedicate your activities to the Lord in the early morning hours. Reflect on the challenges that may come up during the day—at work, at school, with your kids, or in any area of your life—and ask the Lord to give you wisdom to face them.

Think about what your mornings are like. What can you do to start your day with a little more organization? Identify the time you need to get up to start your activities and set an alarm to wake up at least fifteen minutes before that time.

Some people find it more difficult to get up early than others. That's fine. You don't have to become an early riser to be a productive person. The idea is simply that you start the day with some quiet time to reflect on the tasks you have to complete. If you only manage to get up five minutes before work starts, make the most of it. Instead of waking up and looking at your cell phone, spend that time in peace and quiet, asking for wisdom to do your best with new day you have been given.

In summary, set your alarm so you can have some quiet time in the morning to pray and reflect on what you want to accomplish that day.

During the Day

It's time to act. The best way to do this is to remember that everything has its time. The more regularly you use your productivity tools, the more you can rest in the reality that you don't need to worry about the things you're not doing right now because you've planned well and designated specific time for them later.

Try to do one task at a time and not jump from one thing to another. If something is taking a lot of effort, break it down into simpler tasks. For example, instead of studying chapter 5 of a book you could (1) open the book, (2) read two paragraphs, (3) write down the most important idea and read another two paragraphs, and (4) make three notes in the text.

If you don't feel motivated to do something, don't fall into the trap of waiting until you feel like it before doing it. Recognize that you lack motivation and that you do not need to be motivated to have the ability to do something. Step away for a moment (drink a glass of water, walk outside for five minutes, say a prayer) and come back with your eyes fixed on the goal.

If you can, schedule your rest times. It's easy for the fifteen-minute break to turn into an hour of watching videos or wasting time on social media. Allocate specific times to get away from your tasks and make sure that what you do in that time is something that really gives you energy. Eat something healthy, take a nap, drink water, or read something that's educational. The better you nourish your mind, the more energy you will have to perform your activities in the best way.

Remember to identify your energy peaks. Do you work better in the morning, afternoon, or evening? Try to place your creative and demanding tasks in the time slots when you feel most awake and are least likely to be interrupted. If you have children at home, for example, do not try to read while they are on top of you or clean up after they have gone to bed. Rather, get as much of the cleaning done as you can while they are awake and take advantage of the quiet times to do things you need to do without interruptions.

What do we do when our plan is ruined by our procrastination? We keep moving forward. We don't collapse. We can take some time to cry, but we must not remain defeated. We all fall into laziness and procrastination. But productive people recover as fast as they can. Unproductive people feel bad and keep falling. Letting the whole day go to waste just because some things didn't go as expected is the equivalent of eating a whole box of cookies just because you ate one cookie after starting a healthy diet. The world won't end. There's no need to flush the rest of your day down the drain. When I'm in this kind of a situation, I may feel like I'm a failure and that I'm hopeless, but this isn't true. I don't have to solve everything today. I just have to take a deep breath and one small step in the right direction.

If you feel too overwhelmed by your activities, try sitting down and writing out all the things that are on your mind, whatever they are, large or small, pending work or irrational emotion. Don't stop writing until you see every one of those thoughts that crush you on paper. There are things on your list that you won't be able to remedy. Maybe it's some issue that has already happened or decisions that are out of your control. It sounds silly, but crossing them off your list can give you the sense of completion you need in order to focus on what you can solve. Next, identify what really matters.

When I am overwhelmed, everything in my head seems urgent. But when I put it on paper, I realize that there are things I can leave for later. I don't have to work on everything at the same time. It's better to concentrate on one thing and then get on with the rest at another time.

Once you know that the things that were overwhelming you are in a safe place and you won't forget them, you can put them aside temporarily. Check the list again during your next weekly planning session. At that time, concentrate only on what really matters that day. Finally, don't forget to enjoy what you're doing.

Maybe you don't have a lot of money, maybe your job isn't your favorite, maybe your family doesn't appreciate everything you do. Working in a fallen world is painful. However, in the midst of any difficulty, we can rest in the fact that we live to honor a good God who sees our every effort and—even when imperfect—uses it for his glory and the good of our neighbor. No matter how ordinary we may think our activities are, God is using them to restore the world and show the nations who he is. Ask God for a heart that can even enjoy the everyday. Ask him for eyes to see your labors as he sees them.

In summary, focus on one thing at a time, break complex tasks into simple tasks, take productive breaks, take advantage of your energy peaks, get back on track right away, put what overwhelms you on paper, and enjoy life!

At the End of the Day

You have finished your work, congratulations! I'm sure you're exhausted and all you want is a well-deserved rest. You definitely need it. But do your future self a favor: prepare to rest well by making a little effort to plan the next day. Everything has its time, including rest.

And your rest time isn't rest time if you're worried about all the things you have to do tomorrow. These feelings will diminish as you learn to use your productivity tools and get used to reviewing your weekly plan. However, even when we do all these things, it's common to be tempted to worry about the future and all that we have to do. When this happens to me, I try to remember the words of Psalm 127:1–2:

> Unless the LORD builds the house,
>> those who build it labor in vain.
> Unless the LORD watches over the city,
>> the watchman stays awake in vain.
> It is in vain that you rise up early
>> and go late to rest,
> eating the bread of anxious toil;
>> for he gives to his beloved sleep.

Resting is an act of faith. It's an embodiment of the reality that the success of your work doesn't depend on you. What the Christian businessman desires is that the Lord build his business. What the Christian mother desires is for the Lord to take care of her family. We can make great efforts and do our part to diligently fulfill the work that the Lord has entrusted to us. But we can also rest knowing that he is the one who gives us sleep. It's no use wearing yourself out when the God of the universe has everything under control.

We can make great efforts and we can rest. When you rest, do so intentionally, making an effort to avoid the false rest that this superficial world offers. When you're making an effort, do so resting in the fact that the weight of the world isn't on your shoulders. So, when you're done working, stop working. Disconnect from email and household chores (neither of which will ever end), and focus on enjoying the sleep that your loving God gives you.

In summary, when you finish working, stop working, tidy up your work area quickly so that it's ready for tomorrow's work, and make an effort to truly rest in the Lord.

For Reflection

1. What are your mornings like? Do you have quiet time or are they always chaotic? If the latter is the case, what can you do to improve your situation a bit?

2. How do you react when your plans fall apart?

3. Do you find it hard to disconnect from your work when it's time to rest? Why? Think of some simple adjustments you could implement to change this situation.

Action Points

Set a reminder called "Get ready for tomorrow" on your phone. Set it to go off thirty minutes before your bedtime. Make a short list of things you should get ready each night. Here are some ideas:

- Bible
- Coffee
- Sportswear
- Work clothes
- Purse
- Planner

Closing Words

THIS IS JUST THE BEGINNING.

Our time on earth is but an instant compared with eternity. Here our work is stained by sin and hindered by the thorns and thistles of a broken world. As much as we enjoy our labors, they are only a preface to the glorious life of work and rest that we will have in eternity with Christ. We fix our eyes on him as we run the race of faith. We fix our eyes on him as we work to fulfill the mission he has given us.

To make good use of the time is to live in light of the reality of who we already are in Jesus Christ. We have determined to seek wisdom each day for walking as imitators of God, as beloved children, walking in love, just as Christ loved us and gave himself up for us (Eph. 5:1–2). This means that sometimes we work harder and sometimes we stop and rest. Sometimes it will mean saying yes, and at other times it will mean saying no. It might mean focusing on solving a problem at one time and focusing on playing another time. It may mean carefully organizing our daily planner or perhaps leaving the day's schedule completely free.

The wisdom to live well by making good use of time isn't hidden. It's not for a few. Wisdom for living in the right way is available to anyone who cries out for it; if we ask for it in faith, God promises to give it to us (Prov. 1:20–25; James 1:5–8).

This is our call: "'Awake, O sleeper, and arise from the dead, and Christ will shine on you.' Look carefully then how you walk, not as unwise but as wise, making the best use of the time, because the days are evil" (Eph. 5:14–16). Yes, the days are evil. But not for long. Let's make the most of what we have left.

Acknowledgments

To: God
Uriel, Judá, and Hugo
Cecy, Carlos, Fer, and Karla
Iglesia Reforma
Cris Garrido
Jairo Namnún
Cole Brown
Pepe Mendoza
Carol de Rossi
Aixa de López
Valia Lima

Thank you.

General Index

Scripture Index

TGC | THE GOSPEL COALITION

The Gospel Coalition (TGC) supports the church in making disciples of all nations, by providing gospel-centered resources that are trusted and timely, winsome and wise.

Guided by a Council of more than 40 pastors in the Reformed tradition, TGC seeks to advance gospel-centered ministry for the next generation by producing content (including articles, podcasts, videos, courses, and books) and convening leaders (including conferences, virtual events, training, and regional chapters).

In all of this we want to help Christians around the world better grasp the gospel of Jesus Christ and apply it to all of life in the 21st century. We want to offer biblical truth in an era of great confusion. We want to offer gospel-centered hope for the searching.

Through its women's initiatives, The Gospel Coalition aims to support the growth of women in faithfully studying and sharing the Scriptures; in actively loving and serving the church; and in spreading the gospel of Jesus Christ in all their callings.

Join us by visiting TGC.org so you can be equipped to love God with all your heart, soul, mind, and strength, and to love your neighbor as yourself.

TGC.org

Also Available from the Gospel Coalition

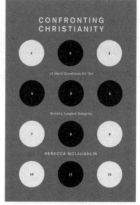

For more information, visit **crossway.org**.